G000088346

A Feast
of
West Sussex

A FEAST OF WEST SUSSEX

Summersdale Publishers Ltd
46 West Street
Chichester
West Sussex
PO19 1RP
UK

www.summersdale.com

Printed and bound in the Czech Republic

ISBN: 978-1-84953-443-7

Substantial discounts on bulk quantities of Summersdale books are available to corporations, professional associations and other organisations. For details contact Nicky Douglas by telephone: +44 (0) 1243 756902, fax +44 (0) 1243 786300 or email: nicky@summersdale.com.

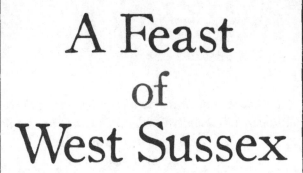

A Feast
of
West Sussex

Rosemary Moon

summersdale

This book is dedicated to all my friends at the Tangmere Community Garden, who have made me realise afresh how important it is to share good food

Contents

Introduction

The writing of this book has turned into a delicious trip through the memories and flavours of thirty years of food writing. For all of that time I have been based here in West Sussex. I have revisited not only local foods, and the people and stories behind them, but favourite recipes too. These are recipes that I know you will like as they have been devoured at my cookery demonstrations around the county.

The most exciting thing about collecting my recipes together has been the realisation of just how much the local food scene in West Sussex has changed, especially over the past decade. The foods on offer now are much more varied and of much better quality. I have concentrated on recipes using locally sourced ingredients, from wherever you shop, for you to make at home, but there are now convenience foods and ready meals being made in the county, full of provenance-rich ingredients, for days when there is no time to cook.

There is no list of growers, retailers and restaurants specialising in local foods within these pages. That list will be kept up to date on a companion website at feastofwestsussex.co.uk. Do look at that for all the extra information that you might need to truly enjoy *A Feast of West Sussex*.

Rosemary Moon
March 2014

Fruit &
Vegetables

Apples

*Tree-ripened season August–October;
stored apples available until March*

Top fruit by name and top fruit by nature, small West Sussex orchards produce this most quintessentially British of fruits. The increasing popularity of imported apple varieties such as Jazz and Fuji has challenged most of our once commercial larger apple farms out of business. Now Sussex-grown apples are very much a crop of community orchards, private gardens, and a few specialist growers producing fruit for farm shops and for juice.

The most comprehensive collection of apples that are native to the county or thrive here is at West Dean Gardens near Chichester. In the orchard, which is now some 20 years old, is a fine collection of heritage varieties. Crawley Beauty and Forge are both local dual-purpose apples, and Doctor Hogg is our only Sussex-bred cooker. Forge was once promoted as the apple tree of choice for cottage gardens throughout the south-east. A favourite of mine is the Tinsley Quince, a delicious eating apple.

Petworth remains our most famous Mecca for apple pilgrims, for it is here that the Egremont Russet was raised on Lord Egremont's estate in the 1870s. The most commercial of all russets (a name given to the khaki-coloured, slightly knobbly skin type on dessert apples) and my favourite eating apple, the Egremont Russet does cook too. I add it to Bramleys or the lesser-known, but just as delicious, Howgate Wonder when cooking pies and crumbles. Diced and tossed in butter, the russet holds its shape well amidst the fluff of the cookers, giving sweetness and texture to apple puds and desserts.

Smaller growers and orchards supplying local fruit through farm shops and farmers' markets have a trump card to play. The immediacy of availability after picking is crucial for early apples such as Discovery, which need to be eaten within two or three days of picking to be at their very best. Farm shops picking for customer demand can specialise in this tight quick-to-market schedule. Discovery is considered by many to be essential in a good mixed juice, to be consumed fresh, or fermented into cider.

The growth of community orchards in West Sussex delights me – and it's not just the fruit, as our county without apple blossom is impossible to imagine.

Chilli Jelly

Makes about 5 x 500g jars

Most flavoured jellies are made on an apple jelly base. This is a great way of using up windfalls – you only need to cut out really bad bits and creepy crawlies! I don't throw the skimmings away but add them to the next spicy dish that I make, be it a stew, curry, etc.

2kg cooking apples
3–4 dried chillies or 1–2 tsp chilli flakes
200ml cider vinegar
15–20 fresh chillies
1kg granulated sugar (approx.)

1. Wash the apples and chop them roughly, then cook them slowly with the dried chillies in 1 litre of water until very soft and reduced to a pulp.

2. Cool slightly, then spoon into a suspended jelly bag and drain overnight. Don't squeeze the bag or this pale coloured jelly will be cloudy.

3. Wash some jars and set them in a warm oven to dry. Chill a small plate in the fridge, and seed and finely chop the fresh chillies. Add the vinegar to the apple juice, then measure it into a large pan and add the chillies with 500g sugar to every 500ml liquid. Bring to the boil, stirring until the sugar is dissolved, then boil rapidly until setting point is reached – the jelly will coat

a wooden spoon and a little placed on the cold plate will wrinkle when pushed with your finger.

4. Skim the surface of the jelly to remove any scum, taking care not to remove too many chillies, then leave for 20–30 minutes before pouring into warmed jars. Cover, seal and label.

5. Leaving the jelly will, as with marmalade, ensure that the fresh chilli is distributed throughout and doesn't rise to the top of the jars.

St Clement's Apple Pie

Serves 8–10

Apple pie is a national treasure, but my West Sussex version is a special occasions pie!

2 lemons
1 orange
4 Egremont Russet eating apples
1kg Bramley or Howgate Wonder cooking apples
25g butter
125g granulated sugar
350g plain flour
1 tbsp caster sugar, plus extra for sprinkling
175g butter
Milk for glazing

1. Finely grate the zest from the lemons and orange. Squeeze the juice of ½ a lemon into a large bowl of water. Squeeze the juice from the remaining lemon halves and the orange, and set to one side. Peel, core and quarter the apples, and place in the water to stop them going brown.

2. Dice the eating apples. Melt the butter in a large pan, add the apple dice and cook for 2–3 minutes. Slice the cookers into the pan, add the sugar, then cover and cook until just holding their shape. Stir in the citrus zest and juice, and add extra sugar to taste if you wish. Set to one side until required.

3. Preheat the oven to gas mark 6/200°C. Mix the flour and caster sugar in a large bowl then add the butter in small pieces and rub the butter and flour between your fingertips until it all resembles fine crumbs. I do this by hand but you could use a mixer or a food processor. Add sufficient cold water to make a stiff dough.

4. Lightly knead ⅔ of the pastry into a smooth-sided round – if you don't it will crack as you roll it. Roll out on a lightly floured surface and use to line the base and sides of a 20cm gateau tin or loose-bottomed tin. Spoon in the apple filling.

5. Roll the remaining pastry out into a circle a little larger than the tin. Dampen the edges of the pastry in the tin with water, then cover with the pastry lid, gently pressing the two together. Trim the edges, then seal them together with little strokes of a knife. I make an

edge by pressing the pastry between the forefinger of my right hand, and the thumb and forefinger of my left. Make a slit in the centre of the pie with a sharp knife. Roll out the pastry trimmings and cut leaves for decoration, placing them round the slit. Brush the decorated pie top with milk.

6. Bake for 35–40 minutes until golden brown. Sprinkle the pie with caster sugar before serving. I bake my apple pies on the floor of the roasting oven of my Aga, which cooks the bottom crust beautifully. Try placing a baking sheet in a conventional oven when preheating and then bake the pie on that for similar results.

Asparagus

April–June

West Sussex is an almost perfect area for growing asparagus. This harbinger of early summer can withstand a salinity of soil that prevents weeds from flourishing for easy harvesting, as it was originally a coastal crop. Asparagus is a long-term investment, yielding a crop over many years as, like rhubarb, the crowns stay in the ground for about 15 seasons.

We are hard on asparagus. We keep cutting off its edible and delicious shoots for our gastronomic pleasure, and it kindly vents its frustrations by producing more and more in a bid to establish itself above ground until, some eight to ten weeks later, it gives up and pushes up fronds of fern in an act of submission and exhaustion! I love to gorge on the local crop until around Midsummer's Day, the traditional end of the season, and then I abstain until the next glorious Sussex crop.

Each crown will throw spears of varying sizes or grades, so thick jumbo spears for soup making will be

16

harvested at the same time from the same plant as fine spears. I never mind which grade of asparagus I buy but I do want all the spears in the bundle to be the same size, so that the cooking will be straightforward. I suggest that you turn your selected bundles upside down and check for uniformity before you buy, for ease of kitchen preparation.

You will need a real passion for asparagus or a very large garden or allotment to put aside enough land for a family-sized harvest. The ferns which grow up after the crop are very decorative and, if you live in the country, can provide good cover for nesting field mice. Once the ferns have withered and dried they can be incorporated into the soil of the asparagus bed, to build disease resistance in the following year's crop.

The gastro-norm was to eat steamed asparagus with hollandaise sauce, but few have an asparagus steamer these days. What has been a revelation to me is griddling and roasting the spears, both methods producing well-cooked asparagus for contemporary cuisine. Snap the ends off to avoid any woodiness (unless you want them as a 'handle' to hold your asparagus by) – these are great in stocks.

Chicken, Ham and Asparagus Pie

Serves 4–6

I love a good pie and they are trendy again. Make things easy for yourself by using prepared pastry if you wish – you could even use canned condensed soup instead of making a sauce. Shortcuts or not, with asparagus, ham and chicken in the filling your pie will be delicious.

　　1 bunch asparagus
　　Oil, e.g. olive or rapeseed
　　50g flour
　　50g butter
　　500ml milk
　　300g cooked chicken
　　300g ham
　　100g cold butter
　　200g plain flour
　　Beaten egg or milk to glaze

1. Preheat the oven to gas mark 6/200°C. Place a 1.5-litre pie dish on a baking tray.

2. Snap off and discard the ends of the asparagus, place the spears in a small roasting tin, season lightly and drizzle with oil. Roast in the pre-heated oven for 10–15 minutes, until just tender, shaking once or twice. Leave to cool.

3. Heat the flour and butter with the milk in a pan over a medium heat, stirring all the time, until blended and thickened into a smooth sauce. Leave to cool.

4. Rub the cold butter into the flour with a pinch of salt until it resembles fine crumbs. Bind the pastry together with just enough cold water to give a firm dough. Lightly chill until required.

5. Chop the chicken, ham and asparagus into bite-sized pieces. Combine in the cooled sauce. Season to taste and pile into the pie dish.

6. Lightly knead the pastry into a smooth ball, then roll out to cover the pie. Make a slit in the centre with a sharp knife, then brush the pastry with milk or beaten egg. Bake in the hot oven for 30 minutes, until the pastry is golden brown. Serve immediately, or let it go cold. Do not reheat the pie as it is made with cooked meats.

Griddled Asparagus and Bean Salad

Serves 4

Griddled asparagus is the star in this light, main course salad.

2 bunches asparagus
1 tsp olive oil
1 red onion
1 red chilli
Small bunch flat-leaf parsley
400g can flageolet beans
Extra virgin olive oil

1. Snap the ends off the asparagus and place the spears on a plate. Drizzle with the olive oil. Prepare the remaining vegetables. Finely chop the red onion, chilli and parsley. Drain and rinse the beans in a sieve and shake dry.

2. Heat a ridged griddle pan or large frying pan until hot. Add the asparagus and cook over a medium heat, turning occasionally, until the spears are just tender. This will take about 8 minutes for medium thickness spears. Transfer to a plate and leave to cool.

3. Mix together the onion, chilli, parsley and beans in a bowl. Chop the thick stalks from the asparagus, leaving the spears about 10cm long. Roughly chop the ends and add them to the bowl. Mix well, season with salt and pepper, and moisten the salad with some extra virgin olive oil.

4. Serve the asparagus spears with the bean and asparagus salad to one side.

Chillies

*August–October; glasshouse crops will be
a little earlier*

Some are hot, some are not, but most of them can be
found in the summer months in the glasshouses at West
Dean Gardens. I'm talking chillies, and this Chichester
centre of horticultural excellence has exploded our
awareness of the Scoville scale (the chilli heat index) in
food and cooking. Through summer-long displays and
the now world-famous Chilli Fiesta held each August in
the otherwise tranquil parkland setting, West Dean is the
place of pilgrimage for anyone seeking chilli knowledge,
plants or products.

I have cooked at the Chilli Fiesta almost every year
since it began in 1996 and I am still coming up with new
recipes to show the flavour and heat variations between
different cultivars in various stages of ripeness. Broadly
speaking, red, orange and yellow are ripe colours, while
green and purple are unripe. Ripe chillies have a deeper,

fruitier flavour, and unripe ones are fresher, crisper and more herbaceous on the tongue. Pick your chilli according to your dish. To see how hot they are, cut one across about a third of the way from the tip (i.e. the other end from the stalk) and then just touch the cut surface to your tongue for an indication of how much chilli to use. Too hot? Drink milk, not beer or water. The fatty particles in milk are much more effective in neutralising the heat (think yogurt raitas with curries). Heat alone, it has been said, is a Man Thing, whereas heat and flavour are culinary sensations to share!

West Dean is not, of course, just about chillies – the Walled Kitchen Gardens are but one part of a large and beautiful estate just waiting to be explored – but they are the essential destination that excites me most as a cook. Serried rows of perfect produce and 13 restored Victorian glasshouses full of trophy-like fruits and vegetables cannot but inspire the home kitchen gardener. It is my idea of horticultural heaven. It is a place to spend a whole day, to look, to sit, to walk, to eat and drink, and to be inspired. But be warned – for three days in August it is given over to chilli-heads, and they are a breed apart!

Pigeon Breasts With Hot Chillies, Cool Peppers and Apple Raita

Serves 2–3

You can use any poultry breasts in this recipe – chicken, pheasant, partridge, or the duck breast mini fillets from supermarkets. I have chosen to use pigeon as they abound in West Sussex, are really quick to cook, and, are very delicious. Find them at farmers' markets or ask a butcher-cum-game dealer to get them for you if you can't source them from a supermarket. The blend of hot chillies and cool peppers works really well with the richness of the meat and the coolness of the yogurt.

For the raita:

  1 tsp cumin seeds
  1 lime
  1 Russet or red apple
  150g natural yogurt
  Pinch of cayenne pepper

For the pigeon breasts:

  1 green pepper

3–4 tomatoes
Small piece of root ginger
2 hot green chillies
1 onion
1 clove garlic
1 tbsp curry paste, preferably one with lime or tamarind
4 pigeon breasts or 225g duck breast mini fillets
1 tbsp groundnut oil or ghee

1. For the raita, heat a large deep frying pan, add the cumin seeds and dry-fry for a few seconds. Turn them into a bowl and take the pan off the heat. Add the grated zest and juice of half the lime, then grate the apple, skin-on, into the bowl and toss in the juice. Add the yogurt with salt and cayenne pepper to taste, and set to one side.

2. Slice the pepper and chop the tomatoes. Peel and roughly chop the ginger, chop the onion and garlic, and seed and chop the chillies, then blend them with the curry paste. Slice the pigeon breasts into strips.

3. Heat the pan again, add the oil and the onion paste, and fry for 3–4 minutes over a medium heat. Increase the heat, add the pigeon and stir-fry for 2 minutes. Add the peppers and tomatoes, and cook for a further 3 minutes. Season to taste with salt. Serve with the apple raita. Pigeon is best if it is not over-cooked – but I don't like it too pink.

Ratatouille with Chillies

Serves 6

I really like the texture achieved by cooking a ratatouille in this way. Try it cold, with melon balls added about an hour before serving – delicious!

1 large aubergine
300–400g courgettes
1 large onion
2 red peppers
2–3 red chillies
1 large clove garlic
1kg fresh tomatoes or 2 x 400g cans chopped tomatoes
150ml olive oil plus extra to garnish

1. Prepare the vegetables. Cut the aubergine and courgettes into similar-sized dice, about 1½cm. Slice the onion and peppers, and finely chop the chillies and garlic. Plunge the fresh tomatoes into boiling water for 30 seconds, or hold them on a fork over a gas flame until the skins split. Refresh in cold water, then peel and chop them finely.

2. Heat a large deep frying pan, add the oil and fry the aubergine until it is browned on all sides. It will yield some of the oil back into the pan as it cooks. Remove the aubergine with a slotted spoon to a plate, then fry

the courgettes until browned all over in the remaining oil. Remove the courgettes from the pan and add to the aubergine.

3. Lower the heat, add the onion to the pan and cook slowly for 6–8 minutes, until soft but not browned. Add the chillies, garlic, peppers and tomatoes and cook for 2–3 minutes, until the peppers are slightly softened. Return the aubergine and courgettes to the pan. Season well and cook for a further 5–8 minutes, or until the vegetables are cooked to your liking and the tomatoes are slightly reduced to a sauce. Season and drizzle with extra virgin olive oil before serving.

Currants

July–August

Currant affairs revolve around the black or red-fruited varieties for me: I haven't quite got white currants because the colour doesn't really add anything to my cooking. I may be wrong, but my first attraction to currant cuisine is through the vibrant colour of the finished dishes.

Without doubt the preparation of currants has to be the discouraging factor for most of us. The easiest way to string them off the clusters in which they grow is with a fork, but that still means you have to check for leftover tiny stalks, and it really is best if you pinch out the remains of the flower heads from the currants too. That said, it's all very therapeutic work and if you can sit and natter as you go it is soon accomplished. I grow three varieties of redcurrants at home, to spread the harvest and the labour, and I grow them trained on a north-facing wall to make the most of my gardening opportunities. This also helps to spread the crop over an even longer period. Blackcurrants cannot be trained, however, and come thick, fast, big, and

27

juicy on what turn into quite large bushes. You need space in a garden for them, but the payback is terrific and it is not only the currants that can be used in the kitchen.

In terms of culinary inspiration I think of redcurrants as English cranberries: the flavour hit is similar. I use them in cakes and bakes, in salads and relishes, and in jam and cordials too. Being off-centre of a mainstream crop, it is again the smaller growers who are keeping our currant options alive by growing for farm shops. There is so much more to redcurrants than summer pudding, a favourite though it is. Blackcurrants make fabulous sorbet, cordial and jam, but I also love to purée them simply into a sauce, to serve with ice cream or to ripple into it. Larger growers in other counties have started making dessert sauces and cordials with their freshly picked fruits, to diversify as currants become more and more a speciality crop. Thankfully some of our West Sussex growers are keeping currants on our menus through their farm shops and fruit-and-veg box schemes.

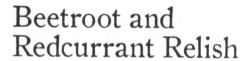

Beetroot and Redcurrant Relish

Serves 6

A no-cook tangy relish for sausages, burgers, chops, ham or chicken. It's also great as part of a salad buffet, and makes the most of redcurrants in a quick and easy way.

250g cooked beetroot
150g redcurrants
Chopped parsley, coriander or a few spring onion tops
1 tsp cumin seeds
1–2 tsp vinegar, balsamic, red wine or fruit

1. Peel and finely chop the beetroot: use a packet of cooked beetroot if you wish, but not the vinegary sort. String the currants by pulling a fork downwards over the fruit from the top of the string. Finely chop the herbs or onion tops.
2. Mix the prepared ingredients with the cumin seeds and vinegar, then add salt, pepper and sugar to taste before serving.

Baked Redcurrant Cheesecake

Serves 10–12

Definitely a pud for adults because of the sharp surprise of the currants in the creamy sweetness of the cheesecake crumb. This is one of my summer favourites. Retro, it even has a biscuit base!

250g redcurrants
200g digestive biscuits

100g crumbly or mild cheese, Duddleswell is
great in this
3 large eggs
150ml double cream
100g butter
175g caster sugar
200g crème fraiche
1 orange
50g plain flour

1. Preheat the oven to gas mark 3/160°C. Top and tail the redcurrants. Crush the digestive biscuits into fine crumbs and grate the cheese. Separate the eggs, placing the yolks and whites in separate large mixing bowls. Lightly whip the cream.

2. Melt the butter, add the biscuit crumbs and 50g of the sugar. Mix well and press into the base of a 23cm springform, loose-bottomed tin. Chill while making the filling.

3. Beat the crème fraiche into the egg yolks. Grate in the zest from the orange, then squeeze the juice and add that too, along with the cheese, flour and whipped cream. Mix, then gently stir in the redcurrants.

4. Whisk the egg whites until stiff – tip the bowl upside down and the egg whites will remain stiff in the bowl if they are ready. Gradually whisk in the remaining caster sugar to make a meringue. Using a hand whisk or a metal spoon, fold the egg whites into the cheese and currant mixture. Pile the filling into the tin over the biscuit base and level the top gently.

5. Bake in the preheated oven for 1½ hours, until well risen and firm to the touch. Turn the oven off, leave the door open and the cheesecake in the oven for 1 hour. It will sink back, but that's OK.

6. Allow the cheesecake to cool completely and chill lightly for an hour or so. Remove from the tin and dust with icing sugar before serving.

Blackcurrant Leaf Sorbet

Serves 6

Making the most of a plant is very satisfying! The leaves of a blackcurrant bush have plenty of flavour in them for a sorbet, which is delicious with summer pudding.

20 blackcurrant leaves
1 lemon
175g caster sugar
1 egg white

1. Remove the stalks then shred the leaves into a bowl. Add 500ml of hot, but not boiling, water, cover and leave to steep for at least an hour.

2. Zest the lemon into a pan, then squeeze the juice into the leaf liquor. Strain into the pan over the zest and

add the sugar. Bring to the boil, stirring until the sugar is dissolved, then boil for 5 minutes. Allow to cool completely, then chill for 2–3 hours.

3. Lightly whisk the egg white until frothy and add to the chilled syrup. Turn into a freezer box and freeze, stirring every 30–60 minutes, or freeze-churn in an ice cream maker until almost frozen. Serve immediately, or turn into a freezer box and freeze until hard.

Posh Jam Tart

Serves 6

Adding blackcurrants and no sugar makes this a little on the sharp side, but it's very delicious. We actually mopped some cheese round in the juices on our plates the first time that I made it, and that was delicious too. It's a perfect way of using up the egg yolk from making the blackcurrant leaf sorbet.

100g cold butter
175g plain flour
1 tbsp caster sugar
1 egg yolk
350g jam
350g blackcurrants, topped if not tailed

1. Cut the butter into small pieces, then rub it into the flour and sugar until it resembles coarse breadcrumbs.

Add the egg yolk and continue mixing, then add a little cold water, if necessary, to bind the pastry together into a firm ball.

2. Knead gently on a lightly floured surface until smooth, then roll out and use to line a 22cm tart tin, preferably with a loose bottom. Chill for 30 minutes while preheating the oven to gas mark 6/200°C. Prick the base of the pastry all over with a fork, line with baking parchment and fill with baking beans, then bake in the preheated oven for 20 minutes.

3. Mix the jam and the blackcurrants together. Remove the beans and paper from the pastry, then pour in the jammy currants and bake for a further 10–15 minutes, until the pastry edge is deeply golden. Leave to cool and set a little before serving – the currants will ooze a lot of juice so the jammy filling will not set firm.

Gooseberries

*June–July; the sweeter dessert varieties
ripen at the end of the season*

Gooseberries are an early-summer treat. From sharp and challenging right through to the sweetest dessert varieties, from green to red but always slightly stripy, they are a cook's delight and a must-have part of summer. My aunt, a clerical wife, told me once that gooseberries and elderflowers are always ready together, six weeks after Easter. They are perfect complementary flavours, made for each other in that joyful serendipitous way of seasonal crops. However, Easter moves from March to April and climate change is now a challenge to early crops of fruit. In the past few years I have found that elderflowers have been ready a good two or three weeks before the first gooseberries, but no gastro-worries: elderflower cordial is just as good with gooseberries as elderflower heads.

Gooseberries provide one of the great alchemy mysteries of the kitchen: why does their jam turn red, from even the greenest of berries, just as setting point is reached? I don't know the answer but it is a perfect indication that the jam is ready for testing for set. As the plants can be trained against even a comparatively shady wall, gooseberries are easy to add into even a small garden for the keen cook, but most people grow them as bushes and run the gauntlet of their thorns while they pick.

Gooseberries, like many fruits, marry well with savoury ingredients as well as with sweet. The first newspaper article ever written about me as a cookery writer featured a recipe for local Sussex mackerel, baked, and served with a sauce of gooseberries stewed with mace and bay leaves, then sweetened slightly before seasoning. It's a super combination of flavours. The berries are also perfect with pork, but it is for desserts and jams that gooseberries are best known.

A difficult commercial crop, because of sawfly and other pests, gooseberries are now typically produced by smaller growers stocking their own shop shelves – and that's certainly true here in West Sussex. Of course, a rich palette of growing will in itself help produce healthier crops, so this is another winning point for the increasing number of people shopping in our county's excellent farm shops.

Gooseberry and Elderflower Jam

Makes about 3kg (8–10 medium jars)

Make this whenever there are plenty of gooseberries – slightly under rather than overripe gives the best results. Use heads of elderflowers or cordial, according to availability.

1½kg green gooseberries
2 lemons
5 heads of elderflowers or 5 tbsp cordial
500ml water
1¾kg granulated sugar

1. Wash, then top and tail the gooseberries into a preserving pan. Relax, that's the hard work done. Finely grate the zests of the lemons into the pan. If you still have elderflowers, tie the heads in a muslin bag – a jelly bag is ideal. Add the elderflowers or cordial to the gooseberries with the water. Simmer for about 30 minutes until the gooseberries are just tender and starting to split.

2. Meanwhile, wash and rinse some jam jars, then place them in the oven at gas mark 3/160°C to dry. Put a plate in the fridge to chill, ready to test for setting.

3. Remove the muslin bag if used, squeezing as much juice as possible from it. Add the sugar to the fruit and

stir until dissolved. Increase the heat and bring to the boil. Boil for 10–15 minutes until the jam starts to turn red, then move the pan off the heat. Spoon a little jam onto the cold plate, leave it for a few seconds then push it with your fingernail. Does it wrinkle? If so, the jam is ready to bottle. If not, boil it for a further few minutes and try again.

4. Skim any creamy crust with a spoon, then pour the jam into the warmed jars and cover. Wipe the jars clean and label them once the jam is cold. Store in a cool, dark cupboard or larder.

Gooseberry and Elderflower Ice Cream

Serves 4–6

Elderflower cordial is used to flavour this light, refreshing ice cream. Making it in a machine achieves a really creamy consistency in what is really almost a sorbet – stir frequently by hand to avoid large ice crystals forming.

500g gooseberries
3 large egg whites
100ml elderflower cordial

100g caster sugar
150ml double cream

1. Cook the gooseberries slowly in a covered pan with 50ml water until soft and starting to split. Press through a sieve and measure the purée – you should have about 400ml. Leave to cool completely then chill.

2. Whisk the egg whites until light and frothy, then add the cold purée and all the remaining ingredients, and combine them with a wire whisk. Turn in an ice cream maker and freeze-churn until ready, or put in freezer in a suitable container, stirring frequently to ensure even, smooth freezing. Eat this ice cream as quickly as possible – within a week. As it is much lower fat than classic ice creams it is more likely to form ice crystals during storage.

Herbs, Cress and Microgreens

The Worthing area has long been famed for its glasshouses and for one crop in particular – mustard and cress, or salad cress as it is now known. I love it for its high notes of mustard oil flavour. I have also been impressed to see the move away from peat in the punnets to recyclable fibrous or paper matting over the past few years.

The great storm of 1987 destroyed many of the cress glasshouses and gave the opportunity to rebuild for a modern industry raising the Mediterranean herbs that were by now so popular, as cheap package holidays had become the norm for summer breaks. Supermarkets now stock a good range of herbs all year round, but it is interesting that Christmas remains a peak sales time for commercial herb growers – as people make their own stuffings for maybe the one and only time of the year.

West Sussex growers are leading the way to the next level of concentrated flavours with the production of pea shoots and microgreens. Originally produced for the catering industry, these tender young bursts of flavour are being grown on ecologically friendly matting without the use of peat. Pea shoots have been such a success in restaurants, especially in risottos, that they are now available in some supermarkets. Of course, you can do your own at home, using either marrowfat peas or pea seeds specially sold by seed companies for sprouting, and they are much better freshly cut than imported in pillow packs, as the current UK growers cannot yet satisfy demand.

Microgreens are tiny little seedlings of anything from kale to garlic chives, mustard leaves to radish and onions, and they are produced in punnets like salad cress. Their flavour is intense, and for dishes that need a kick when chilli and garlic are not in order, this emerging crop is one to look out for.

Sweet Tomato and Pea Salad

This is a salad that doesn't need quantities, except you need to make lots as it is delicious! Adding crumbled feta or a cheese of your choice would make a substantial main course salad.

Baby plum or cherry tomatoes
Petit pois, fresh or frozen
Pea shoots
Extra virgin olive oil

1. Preheat the oven to gas mark 3/160°C and line a baking
   sheet with non-stick parchment. Cut the tomatoes in
   half and place them cut-side up on the baking sheet.
   Sprinkle with salt and sugar then bake for 30–45
   minutes, until semi-collapsed.

2. If using frozen petit pois which are not quite defrosted,
   pour boiling water over them in a colander, then plunge
   into cold water to refresh them. Mix the petit pois with
   pea shoots and dress with olive oil and salt if required.

3. Carefully lift the tomatoes from the parchment. Layer
   them with the dressed petit pois and pea shoots on a
   platter and serve.

Rosemary-Baked Camembert

Serves 2–3

*The cheese for this can be a St George goat's cheese from
East Sussex, an Isle of Wight soft cheese, a Levin Down
from Goodwood or a Somerset Camembert or, indeed,
any whole small soft cheese that you like. This is from an*

idea for a recipe that I wrote for the Fresh Herb Company, based just outside Chichester and in Worthing.

250g soft cheese
Small springs of rosemary
1 clove garlic
1 small red chilli

1. Insert tiny sprigs of 3–5 leaves of rosemary into slits in a whole Somerset Camembert, or soft cheese of your choice. Add garlic slivers and some pieces of chilli too, if you wish.

2. Bake in the wooden cheese box on medium power in a microwave for 3–4 minutes, until the cheese is melted, or in a conventional oven preheated to gas mark 5/190°C for about 8–10 minutes, depending on the ripeness of the cheese. Serve with toast and crudities.

Lavender

July

Lavender might not be the most obvious of culinary ingredients but it is part of summer cooking for me. Fields of the herb – for a herb it most surely is – have a deeply musky, citric and pungent fragrance that always make me think of lemons, as I build imaginary culinary flavour trails. Lavender as a scent seems deliciously old-fashioned – the stuff of calico fresheners for handkerchief and undies drawers. And that has been the problem for the UK lavender growers, how to revamp the image of their crop.

West Sussex's lavender specialists are Lordington Lavender, situated to the west of Funtington near Chichester. Sadly out of sight of the nearby road, farmer Andrew Elms organises open days every July for people to not only to marvel at the sight and scent of the lavender, but also to see the harvest. The scent of the operation is unforgettable.

Lordington produces a culinary essence of lavender which makes contemporary dishes really easy to achieve: add it to creamy desserts such as ice creams and panna cottas, or use it in biscuits and cakes – it's really good in shortbreads with white chocolate. A few bold cheesemakers even add it to their curds, which produces a very different cheese indeed.

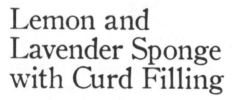

Lemon and Lavender Sponge with Curd Filling

Makes 1 large cake

My must-make-at-least-once-a-summer lavender recipe picks up on the affinity for lemons. Summer on a plate! Use the leftover lavender sugar in biscuits or sprinkle on strawberries.

For the lavender sugar – make this 4–5 days before making the cake:

20 spikes of lavender, picked in full bloom
on a warm, still day
500g caster sugar

1. Strip the flower heads from the stalks, chop them finely, then bury them, preferably in a muslin bag, in the sugar in a sealed container. Shake well and leave for 4–5 days.

For the curd – makes 3–4 small jars:

4 lemons
125g butter
4 large eggs
500g lavender sugar

1. Wash some jars in hot soapy water and scrub off any old labels. Rinse well and put them in an oven at gas mark 3/160°C to dry.

2. Grate the lemon zest finely into a large heatproof bowl, then add the lemon juice. Chop the butter into small pieces and beat the eggs, then add them to the bowl with the sugar.

3. Set the bowl over a pan of hot water, and heat until the sugar is dissolved and the butter melted, then continue cooking, stirring almost constantly, until the curd has thickened and coats the back of the wooden spoon. Alternatively, heat everything together in the microwave cooker for bursts of 1–2 minutes, then stir and return to the microwave. Repeat the heating and stirring until the curd is thick, reducing the length of each cooking period as the mixture thickens.

4. Pour the curd into the warmed jars and cover with lids. Label when cold and keep in the fridge. Use within 1 month.

For the cake:

4 large eggs
200g softened butter or soft baking margarine
200g lavender sugar
225g self-raising flour
1 tsp baking powder

1. Preheat the oven to gas mark 4/180°C. Lightly butter 2 x 20cm sandwich tins and line the bottoms with greaseproof paper or baking parchment.
2. Beat the eggs in a large bowl, then add the butter, sugar, flour and baking powder. Beat thoroughly until combined, then continue beating for a further 1 minute. Add 1 tbsp warm water and beat again – this helps with the rising of a one-stage cake.
3. Divide the mixture between the tins and bake in the centre of the preheated oven for 20–25 minutes, or until the cakes spring back to the touch. Stand for a few minutes, then carefully turn out onto wire racks to cool.
4. Fill with lemon and lavender curd, and sprinkle with caster sugar before serving.

Pears and Plums

Plums: August–September; Pears: September–
October, and stored through to March/April

Always the bridesmaid, never the bride: pears and plums just don't seem to achieve the same dedicated following as apples and both deserve much more of a starring role in our kitchens. Maybe they are just too difficult to deal with? With plums it's a race to the fruit before the wasps, and pears are said to have just one perfect day for sublime enjoyment.

This book is about West Sussex food and so I am going to stick my neck out here and claim Victoria plums for our own. For years reference books have followed each other, naming Alderton in Sussex as the place where the first Victoria plum tree was found and thus perpetuating a possible myth. There is a problem – there's no such place and there are no records of there ever having been one! I am going with the theory that Alderton is actually Walderton, near Funtington – and that is why Funtington is a plum centre of excellence!

Pears are a challenge to grow commercially, as one moment they are as hard as bullets and the next they have ripened a little too far for preserving or cooking. They are best picked firm but almost ripe – and it takes a skilled grower to know when that is. I like to cook with Williams pears, with their perfect filling-bearing 'hips' – the core is easy to hollow out from the base, yielding a cavity to stuff or to ensure perfect poaching. Ripe pears make gorgeous salads with watercress, cheese and crispy bacon or cured meats, as well as the more usual crumbles, tarts and flans. They are also wonderful roasted with partridge, or spiced to serve as a pickle at Christmas. Pear trees are also very agreeable to training, and decorative shapes such as four-winged pyramids and goblets are on show in the orchards at West Dean, and are recommended for small gardens for their stunning blossom and colourful foliage as well as their fruit.

Without doubt the best of these speciality West Sussex-grown fruits will be found in local farm shops and not in supermarkets, or at farmers' markets when the moment is right for the fruit to be magnificent.

Pasta with Plums, Chilli and Basil

Serves 2

This might sound strange but it really works well. Think Chinese; plums, spice – then add pasta.

350g plums
1 clove garlic
2 red chillies
1 green chilli
½ a lemon
2 tbsp fruity olive oil
A pinch of dried chilli flakes
2–3 tbsp double cream
1 tbsp mixed basil leaves, including some Thai
or Greek basil, if possible
Freshly cooked pasta

1. Stone the plums and roughly chop them. Finely chop the garlic with the chillies, after removing their seeds. Squeeze the juice from the lemon.
2. Heat a frying pan, add the oil with the plums and cook until starting to soften in about 4 minutes, then add the garlic, chillies and chilli flakes. Cook to a thick, pulpy sauce.

3. Add the lemon juice to the pan, let it bubble, then add the cream and heat gently. Shred the basil leaves finely and add with salt, pepper and sugar to taste.

4. Toss the pasta in the sauce and serve with a little more basil. I do not think this is a sauce that needs Parmesan, but if you would like to add cheese I suggest a pecorino, which is made from ewe's milk and is slightly sweeter and more complementary for this sauce.

Spiced Plum Salsa

Serves 4

A perfect autumn accompaniment to barbecued meat or fish, sausages or steaks. We also love it with ribs or chicken wings, cooked in a spicy marinade or sauce.

250g plums
1 chilli, red or green
1 small bunch coriander
1 clove garlic
2 spring onions
A few cobnuts, walnuts or blanched almonds
5cm fresh root ginger

1. Stone and chop the plums. Seed the chilli and chop it finely with the coriander and garlic. Slice the onions and roughly chop the nuts.

2. Mix everything together and season. Grate the ginger coarsely with its skin, then gather the shreds in your hand and squeeze the juice over the salsa. Stir and leave to infuse for at least 10 minutes before serving.

Sussex Pear Salad

Serves 2

I have always enjoyed the combination of fruit and spicy meats, and this salad works really well with a pear at perfect ripeness. The pear and the fig are delicious together.

1 ripe fig
1 ripe pear
A handful of watercress or rocket
Thinly cut salami or cured ham
4 roast and marinated artichoke hearts
1 tbsp pistachio kernels or walnuts
Olive oil and balsamic or fruit vinegar to dress

1. Cut the figs into quarters. Cut the pear into quarters or halves and remove the core; I would leave the skin on if the pear is perfectly ripe.

2. Arrange the greenery on 2 plates, then top it with the meat, folded over and curled. Add the fig, pear and artichoke hearts, then scatter the nuts over. Season lightly with salt and pepper.

3. Dress the salad with a good extra virgin olive oil and a few drops of vinegar just before serving.

Campari Poached Pears

Serves 4

Pears poached in red wine is a culinary classic – this is my contemporary twist, which gives a pretty colour to the pears as well as a delicious flavour.

200g granulated sugar
Juice of 1 lemon
75ml Campari
2 tbsp Angostura Bitters
4 Comice or Williams pears, ripe but firm

1. Place the sugar in a small saucepan with 1 litre of cold water and bring to the boil. Stir to dissolve the sugar, then boil quickly for 10 minutes until reduced by ⅓. Add the lemon juice, Campari and Bitters.

2. Trim the bottoms from the pears so that they will sit flat, and scoop out the core – this is easiest with a melon baller. Finally, peel the fruits – they are too slippery to hold and core if you peel them first. Immerse the pears in the syrup, then press a piece of baking parchment or

greaseproof paper over them to keep them submerged, and cover the saucepan with a lid. Poach slowly for 12–15 minutes, or until just tender, then leave the pears to cool in the syrup, off the heat.

3. Remove the pears to a serving dish and chill lightly for an hour or so. Boil the syrup for a further 10 minutes, or until reduced by half. Place the saucepan in a sink of cold water to cool and then serve the syrup poured over the pears. Serve the pears with a fruit sorbet; cream or ice cream smothers their delicate flavour.

Peppers

June–November (glasshouse);
August–September (outdoor)

We love peppers in this country and they are now part of our day-to-day diet. It's a huge turnaround from the dark ages when I was training as a home economist, when package holidays were just becoming popular and we had discovered risotto (then thought to be a dish of easy-cook long-grain rice, chopped green peppers and ham). Times have changed, as has the scale of growing on the coastal plain of West Sussex. The pepper nurseries at Tangmere have evolved over the past 25 years and now the glasshouses cover an area of 30ha (74 acres), the equivalent of 60 football pitches, producing about 40 per cent of the UK crop. It is huge!

All the Tangmere peppers start green, but if left on the plants for a further ten days or so past green pepper maturity the fruits will ripen to yellow, orange or red, according to variety. The riper colours have a sweeter and less herbaceous flavour and they tend to be more popular – our taste buds are definitely seduced by sweetness. I love green peppers in curries and other spicy dishes, but for most recipes the sweeter flavours work well. The real treats from the nursery are the pointed red Romano peppers – often Klingon-like in their ridging towards the stalk but almost oozing sweetness. They are stunning in salsas, stir-fries and frittatas, especially when mixed with chard.

Sweet Pepper, Chard and Chervil Frittata

Serves 3–4

Sweet Romano peppers are perfect with chard, and chervil, which is slightly aniseed, is a great herb to put with them.

10–12 large stems chard
Small bunch fresh chervil, flat-leaf parsley or tarragon
1 Romano pepper
6 large eggs
1 tbsp olive oil
50–75g cheese, Parmesan, feta or whatever you have

1. Pick through the chard, trim the stalks and strip the leaves from them. Wash thoroughly. Slice the stalks

and shred the leaves finely, keeping them separate. Roughly chop the chervil or herbs, and seed then chop the pepper. Grate or finely dice the cheese.

2. Beat the eggs with some salt and pepper and the chervil in a bowl.

3. Heat a non-stick frying pan, add the oil and the chard stalks, and sauté slowly over a medium heat until starting to soften, stirring occasionally.

4. Add the shredded leaves to the pan with the pepper and stir-fry until the chard leaves have wilted.

5. Pour in the beaten eggs and cook over a low to medium heat until almost set, pulling the cooked egg to the outside and allowing the unset egg to run into the centre. Preheat the grill. Scatter the cheese over the almost set frittata, then grill until just set and browned.

6. Leave for a few minutes before cutting. Serve warm or cold but not refrigerated.

◇————◇•◇————◇

Vegetable Bobotie

Serves 6

This is a Cape Malay classic from South Africa, tweaked to be all about veg and not about meat – brilliantly flavoured and very colourful. It is easy entertaining at its best. I usually serve it with a rice salad coloured with turmeric and full of chopped spring onions, a tomato salad and mango chutney.

2 large onions
750g mixed root vegetables
2 green peppers
1cm slice bread
250ml milk
1 lemon
3 tbsp groundnut oil
1 tbsp curry paste
1 tsp ground turmeric
1 tsp salt
1 tbsp Demerara sugar
75g raisins
3 tbsp mango chutney
2 large eggs
50g toasted flaked almonds

1. Preheat the oven to gas mark 4/180°C. Finely chop the onions. Peel then dice or slice the mixed vegetables into ½cm pieces. Seed and chop the peppers. Soak the bread in the milk. Grate the zest from the lemon and squeeze the juice. That's all the hard, time-consuming work done.

2. Cook the onions in the oil in a large frying pan for about 5 minutes until soft. Add the curry paste and turmeric to the onion, and cook for a further 1 minute, then add the diced vegetables except the peppers and fry quickly until starting to brown.

3. Squeeze the bread dry, reserving the milk, and crumble it into the veg off the heat. Add the lemon zest and juice, salt, pepper, sugar, raisins, chutney and 1 egg,

then stir in the raw chopped peppers. Pack the mixture into a suitable buttered dish and cover with foil. Bake for 1½ hours.

4. Increase the oven temperature to gas mark 6/200°C. Scatter the almonds over the bobotie. Measure the reserved milk and add a little extra, if necessary, to give 250ml. Add the remaining egg, beat well and pour the mixture over the almonds. Bake for 20 minutes.

5. Serve the Bobotie with a rice and onion salad, a tomato salad and mango chutney.

Potatoes

Year round, including from store; new
potatoes: June–July

Potatoes: they are not the first crop to spring to mind as produce of West Sussex, but they have a key role to play here in crop rotation in our fabulously fertile land. Our specialist growers rent land from other farmers for a season and, after harvest, the fields need fewer inputs for the following crop, the soil structure has been opened up or loosened by the tubers, the potato farmer has a clean crop and it's a win-win situation.

Choosing the right variety for your land is important, not only for yield but also to avoid scab and other underground pest problems, as well as blight. Most allotment growers will do well with Charlottes or Rockets, which are out of the ground and devoured long before the common potato pests need attention. They also prepare the land brilliantly for a follow-on crop of leeks. Within the county we can buy local Marfona, a fabulous all-round variety which bakes brilliantly; King Edward, possibly the ultimate roasting potato, especially when shaken in the pan after par-boiling to roughen up the edges, making it crispier after roasting; and Saxon and Mozart. The latter two are perhaps less well-known varieties. Mozart is a red potato, waxy and wonderful in potato salads, with Saxon actually being a second early, or New potato, variety but a delicious multi-purpose spud which seems to keep well for baking.

Potatoes are in danger of becoming a 'too-hard-to-deal-with' ingredient. I have a niece who amazed us by announcing that she is just too busy to peel them, favouring rice and pasta which go straight from packet to boiling water. Prepared mashed potato sells in absolutely enormous volumes in supermarkets at Christmastime but I don't think anything comes close to home-made mash. I catered for a wedding once where the main course was bangers and mash, and the sight of huge trays of West Sussex potatoes, creamed with milk and butter and baked under a crust of gold, almost moved the groom's friends – and his father's generation too – to riot in the buffet queue. Getting creative with West Sussex potatoes as a contemporary cook is a delicious challenge.

Potato Salad

How did we ever lose sight of the deliciousness of potato salad? A fine salad of waxy tubers is a treat in the spring, before the new potatoes arrive. Use chives all year round and wild garlic in season. You don't need quantities for this recipe – make lots as it keeps well in the fridge, although the salad is at its most sublime at room temperature having never been chilled.

Waxy potatoes – e.g. Mozart
Mayonnaise
Natural yogurt
3–4 gherkins (optional)
3–4 stalks and flower heads of wild garlic
or a handful of chives

1. Peel the potatoes and cut them into 1–2cm dice. Cook in boiling water for 10 minutes or until tender.

2. Mix equal quantities of mayonnaise and yogurt together in a bowl and season. Drain the potatoes and cool for 5 minutes, then add them, warm, to the dressing. Toss well and leave to cool. Slice or dice the gherkins and finely chop the garlic stalks and any unopened flower heads or chives. Add them to the cooled salad, then garnish with any open flowers of wild garlic or chives, just before serving.

Potato and Pea Curry with Cheese

Serves 3–4

A favourite curry to serve in place of rice with other curries, or with hot or cold meat or fish. It's a real treat with new potatoes and fresh peas in June.

2 large onions
1 clove garlic
4–5cm piece root ginger
1 red chilli
500g potatoes
3 tomatoes
2 tbsp ghee or oil
1 tbsp Amarillo chilli powder, 2 tsp ground coriander
and 1 tsp ground ginger; or 1–2 tbsp
curry paste or powder, to taste
300g frozen petit pois
200g cheese, Sussex High Weald halloumi,
Cornish Yarg or Indian paneer
Mint to garnish

1. Prepare the vegetables. Roughly chop the onions, garlic and peeled ginger, and place in a blender. Seed the chilli, add it to the onions and blend them together to a purée. Set to one side. Scrub or peel the potatoes and cut them into 3–4cm pieces. Roughly chop the tomatoes.

2. Melt the ghee in a frying pan, add the onion paste and the spices, and cook slowly over a low heat while the potatoes cook, stirring occasionally.

3. Bring the potatoes to the boil in a pan of water, then simmer for 10 minutes. Add the peas, return to the boil and cook for 3 minutes. Add the tomatoes to the onions as you add the peas to the potatoes. Drain the peas and potatoes, then return them to the pan.

4. Season the onion mixture with salt, then pour it over the potatoes. Cover and cook for 2–3 minutes, until the potatoes are cooked through, then season again.

5. Chop the cheese into 1cm cubes. Sussex halloumi will keep its shape, more like the Indian paneer, whereas Yarg will melt. Add the cheese to the pan, leave for 1 minute to heat or melt slightly, then serve, garnished with mint.

Pumpkins and Squashes

September–November

There's culinary light beyond the lanterns! I love this weird and wonderful-looking family of vegetables. I seem to spend October and November each year persuading people to buy pumpkins for more than just Halloween and not to throw away the flesh scooped out of spooky-faced shells. I've even cooked them on BBC One's *Countryfile* with Matt Baker – squashing up to him was fun!

Pumpkins and squashes are *Cucurbita*, the same family as cucumbers, courgettes and melons. They are divided into summer and winter varieties according to the thickness of their skins, and therefore their keeping qualities. Gem squash, the small dark-green globes and big orange pumpkins have softer skins and need to be eaten before varieties like Crown Prince (my favourite

64

squash). This has a hard grey skin and, if regularly turned, will keep well into the winter.

Cutting into a squash is the biggest problem for most of us. Knobbly Hubbards and the wonderfully sweet and deeply segmented Muscat de Provençe have very hard skins which require a sharp knife or cleaver and plenty of strength to slice through, especially for the first cut. Market stalls and greengrocers have this right, cutting them for sale by the slice, an opportunity to try and taste. Baking them whole before cutting does soften the skin but it also means that the whole vegetable must be used up quite quickly. Butternuts are now very well known and liked, but there is a real danger of them becoming ubiquitous as supermarkets do not offer cut produce. It is therefore a wonderful thing that the West Sussex village of Slindon has become so well known for its pumpkins and all things *Cucurbita* that it now has a Pumpkin Festival at the end of October each year.

Ralph and Barbara Upton of Slindon were pumpkin pioneers in the UK. Every year Ralph would create a dramatic display on their store roof using every type of squash and pumpkin that they grew. Just about every weekend national newspaper supplement featured them. The Uptons personified food lovers for me. They were incredibly generous with their time, experience and knowledge. The business has been carried on by their son Robin, but I still miss Ralph and Barbara, especially at pumpkin time.

Squash Hummus

Serves 4–6

You can make this with or without the chickpeas. I love it both ways so do try it for yourself and decide which way you think is best.

500g Crown Prince squash
400g can chickpeas, drained but liquid reserved
½ tsp ground cumin
3 tbsp tahini
1–2 cloves garlic
100ml extra virgin olive oil, plus a little more

1. Preheat the oven to gas mark 7/220°C. Cut the squash into 2–3cm wedges, and sprinkle with the cumin and a little oil. Roast for 45 minutes or until tender. Leave to cool completely.

2. Scrape the squash from the skin and place in a processor or blender with the chickpeas, tahini and garlic. Blend until almost smooth, adding a little of the reserved liquid from the can, then add the oil until the hummus is the consistency that you like best. Season to taste and serve with toast, pitta or vegetables.

Lamb and Kabocha Pie

Serves 6–8

I originally created this pie for a New Zealander colleague, a lamb man who loved beer and ate lots of squash – it's a very popular veg in New Zealand. Use a Butternut if you cannot find a Kabocha. Southdown lamb is the perfect meat.

8 shallots
1 small Kabocha or Butternut squash
500g diced lamb, leg holds its shape better than shoulder
25g butter
1 tbsp oil
1 tsp ground cumin
2 tbsp oatmeal
250ml beer, Arundel Brewery's Old Knucker
or a similar brown ale
2 bay leaves
350g plain flour
175g butter, or butter and lard mixed

1. Peel the shallots and, if large, cut them in half. Peel, seed and cut the squash into 1–1½cm dice.

2. Heat the butter and oil together in a flameproof casserole, add the shallots and cook quickly until browned, then add the lamb and brown that too. Add the squash and cook, covered, for 2 minutes.

3. Stir in the spice and oatmeal, and cook for a few seconds, then gradually add the beer, stirring all the time. Add a little water, if necessary, to cover the meat and bring to the boil, stirring continuously. Add the bay leaves with some seasoning, then cover and cook slowly for 1½ hours or until tender. Do this on the hob at a slow simmer or in a slow oven at gas mark 3/160°C. Season again when cooked, then allow it to cool completely if possible (it helps to bake the pastry crisper).

4. Preheat the oven to gas mark 6/200°C. Mix the flour with a little salt in a bowl, add the butter or fat cut into small pieces and blend the fat into the flour with your fingertips until it resembles fine crumbs. Bind to a stiff dough with cold water.

5. Lightly form about ⅓ of the pastry into a smooth ball on a lightly floured surface, then roll out to cover the base of a 21–23cm dished pie plate – an enamel one is best. Spoon the lamb and squash mix into the pastry, then roll out the remaining dough and use to cover the filling. Dampen the rim of the bottom crust with cold water, then seal the 2 edges together by pressing them firmly but lightly and crimping them decoratively with your fingers. Use any trimmings to make pastry leaves and use a little water to stick them to the crust. Brush lightly with milk.

6. Bake for 40–45 minutes until the pastry is golden brown and crisp.

Raspberries

June–October; April–November
(glasshouse)

Autumn Bliss. OK, that's a variety of raspberry but it also sums up my feelings about these wonderful berries: happiness! Not sugary sweet, they appeal to my palate as they challenge the taste buds and really deliver on flavour throughout the season.

Raspberries fall into two categories: summer berries, which are borne on canes from the previous season, and autumn berries, which come on the same year's growth. In terms of garden jobs, the earlier berries require the grower to cut out old growth and tie in the canes for next year's fruit. The autumn berries are the easier option: you cut the canes right down each spring, and they grow back and produce fruit the same season. Canes do spread in the fruit patch so need to be kept under control. Any new canes cut out can be stripped of their leaves, which can then be dried, and used for fruit teas.

Some gardeners in the north of West Sussex find their soil doesn't suit summer raspberries and both types do not always grow well in the same area. However, commercial glasshouse growers have pushed the horticultural boundaries in the county yet again, making West Sussex a centre of excellence for the glasshouse production of raspberries for crops in April and November, with field berries fruitfully filling the months in between.

Raspberries are slightly acidic, which is why they bring out the flavours of whatever you serve or cook them with – be it creamy deliciousness or another fruit. In my rhubarb cômpote cooked with star anise, they make the spice of the anise sparkle through all the fruit. They stand up well to strong flavours such as whisky or honey, and raspberries with blackcurrants are incomparable and very colourful.

Any jam maker will tell you that the best preserves are made with just-picked fruit. There are still pick-your-own opportunities for raspberries in the county and jam made with berries picked an hour or so before cooking has the brightest of flavours. Making raspberry jam is quicker than mixing and baking the scones to go with it!

Raspberry Jam

The beauty of raspberry jam for the home gardener or pick-your-own enthusiast is that you can make it with whatever quantity of fruit that you pick – and it truly is worth making even 1 or 2 pots at a time. For quantities more than 400g of fruit I had the finely grated zest of 1 lemon

Equal amounts of raspberries and granulated sugar
Lemon zest

1. Thoroughly scrub and wash some jars and lids. Rinse and set in a warm oven to dry and sterilise. Chill a plate in the fridge.
2. Heat the raspberries in a large pan until the juices start to run. Add the sugar (if you warm it first in a bowl in the oven it will dissolve more quickly) and stir until dissolved.
3. Increase the heat and bring to the boil. Boil the jam for 5 minutes, carefully stirring once or twice. Draw the pan aside, spoon a little jam on to a chilled plate – leave for a few seconds then push it with your finger – if it wrinkles the jam will set. If not, boil for a minute or two longer. Pour the jam into the warmed jars and seal. Label when cool.

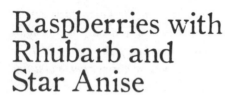

Raspberries with Rhubarb and Star Anise

Serves 4–6

This combination of flavours is a very great favourite in our house. It seems an unlikely pairing of ingredients as rhubarb is a much earlier crop than raspberries. I often make this in the springtime with fresh rhubarb and frozen berries. It is a brilliant mix of complementary flavours.

    4–5 sticks rhubarb
    125g granulated or Demerara sugar
    2 star anise
    300–350g frozen raspberries

1. Slice the rhubarb and cook it in a covered pan with the sugar and star anise for 6–8 minutes, until just softened and starting to break down. The actual cooking time will depend on the age of the rhubarb. Taste and add more sugar if required, then add the frozen raspberries. Stir and cook just until the raspberries have defrosted. Remove the star anise before serving hot or cold. Try this with ice cream, yogurt, or over sponge cake with custard.

Rhubarb

April–August (outdoor)

Rhubarb is a curiously British speciality, being eaten here, in New Zealand, and just a few other countries of the Commonwealth where British influence still lingers. Even in Holland, the source of much of the early-season crop, there is little market for the actual product. If Yorkshire has laid claim to forced rhubarb then West Sussex has a reasonable right to declare outdoor rhubarb as its own. Our early-season sunshine certainly brings the crop on well and, with it, the hope of spring not too far away.

Forced and outdoor rhubarb really need to be treated as separate crops. The former, Barbie-pink in colour and tender from lack of light, is nibbled raw and not always dipped in sugar by the crop's real hard-core fans. It is bright in flavour, but the outdoor crop, for me, is longer lasting on the palate. Outdoor has the winter weather to contend with. Many crops that grow in challenging

73

circumstances develop a greater depth of flavour as a result of their determined struggle to fruition. Like an unpasteurised cheese, the flavour of outdoor rhubarb develops in the mouth and lingers – a burst of gastro-brightness after the muted tastes of winter.

I am avoiding calling rhubarb a fruit: it is in fact a vegetable of Chinese origin, and for centuries it was only used dried and ground into powder in Chinese medicines. It was the Victorians who really got a taste for the fresh sticks, beginning to breed new cultivars with names that reflect the times, including Victoria and Early Albert.

For many non-seasonal cooks rhubarb is an almost unknown ingredient. Perhaps some fear of the sugar often required to sweeten it? Chopping sweet cicely leaves into the pan with the rhubarb when cooking it cuts down the amount of sugar required quite significantly. Being a vegetable, rhubarb does actually cook brilliantly in many savoury dishes: it is fabulous with pork, makes a wonderful sauce with Chinese-style lamb and, when cooked with orange, is great with pork, duck, sausages, and oily fish such as mackerel and salmon. It also makes great chutney. All in all, it's a pretty perfect ingredient.

Chinese-Style Lamb with Rhubarb

Serves 4–6

I have cooked this mix of ingredients as a roast and as a casserole: it is delicious both ways, according to your cut of meat. To roast, have the butcher remove the blade bone from a shoulder, and fill the cavity with the vegetables and seasonings.

4 large sticks rhubarb
2 large onions
2 cloves garlic
100g preserved or crystallised ginger
750g diced lamb, leg holds its shape best,
shoulder is sweeter
2 tsp Chinese 5 spice
3–4 tbsp sweet soy sauce
Freshly chopped salad onions and coriander to garnish

1. Finely slice the rhubarb, dice the onions, crush the garlic and finely chop the ginger.
2. Heat a flameproof casserole until hot, add the lamb and cook quickly on all sides to colour. Add the Chinese 5 spice, stir and cook again for 1 minute, then add the prepared ingredients. Cover and cook slowly for 20 minutes, stirring once.

3. Add the soy sauce and 1–2 tbsp syrup if using preserved ginger, plus sufficient water to barely cover the meat. Cover again and simmer for about an hour, until the lamb is tender, or for longer if it suits you (casseroles are so tolerant).

4. Season to taste, either with salt or more soy sauce. Reduce the sauce slightly if necessary by boiling hard after removing the meat from the pan. Return the lamb to the sauce and serve, garnished with onions and coriander.

Toffee Rhubarb Jacks

Makes 12

I am a great fan of flapjacks and love adding fruit to the basic mix. You can make this with regular porridge oats and add in some raisins, dried cranberries or dried apple rings, all finely chopped. I would suggest 350g oats and 100g fruit. I have made it here with fruit porridge. This is more of a muesli bar than a flapjack, but it's very good.

3 sticks rhubarb, about 300g
150g butter
150g Demerara sugar
450g fruit porridge (see above for alternatives)

1. Preheat the oven to gas mark 6/200°C. Line a shallow baking tin (approx. 18 x 28cm) with baking parchment. The size is not critical, but a deeper mix in a smaller tin will need a longer bake.

2. Slice the rhubarb. Cook with as little water as possible – just 2–3 tbsp – until soft. Do this in a saucepan or a microwave. Stir, add the butter and sugar, and heat again gently until the butter has melted and the sugar dissolved.

3. Stir in the porridge and dried fruit, then spread the mixture out evenly in the tin. Bake for approx. 25 minutes until golden, or until firmly set to the touch.

4. Cut into fingers or squares as soon as it comes out of the oven, then cut it a couple more times as it cools in the tin. I store this in the fridge because of the fresh rhubarb in it.

Salads

All year

A catch-all phrase for the green stuff in our salad bowls. Be it traditional round lettuces, cucumbers, rocket, curly and colourful leaves or crispy golden ones, they are all grown here in West Sussex and we produce lettuce all year round, either in glasshouses or outdoors.

The first crops of Sweet Romaine lettuces, the essential ingredient of the now ubiquitous Caesar salad, were grown on the Chichester plain. Indeed I met the mother of my godson, the grower of the first Romaines, when she asked me to write a recipe leaflet to help market the crop. These truly sweet leaves have challenged our perception of lettuce, and we should all steer clear of imitation Caesars made with other cultivars as they completely miss the point of this truly delicious salad.

Although the popularity of rocket has challenged many of our traditional salad crops, the plant is not new to West Sussex. In the sixteenth and seventeenth centuries it was in common use in English semi-wild salads. Today I think the best local rocket and peppery salad mixes come from market gardeners selling in farmers' markets and through their own vegetable box schemes. Like so many other fruits and vegetables, the flavour is best as soon after harvest as possible, so these are also great to grow at home, even if just in a pot on a sunny windowsill.

Use your lettuce fresh and it will not have a chance to go brown. However, commercial growers stop watering iceberg lettuces up to ten days before harvest to prevent the browning of prepared bagged salads – fascinating information for the home grower. And a top tip: use your cucumbers quickly and don't leave them for longer than a day or two in the fridge, as chilling turns them back to water.

⟡•⟡

Sea Bass Caesar

Serves 2–3 as a main course, 4–6 as a starter

Romaine lettuce is the essential ingredient in this salad for the sweet, crisp base. The original Caesar salad recipe suggested using very lightly boiled eggs for the dressing – a salmonella nightmare! I am using raw egg yolk but you could use about 250ml mayonnaise if you prefer. Do, however, mix it with yogurt or cream to soften the flavour. I have used bought croutons, but make your own if you have the time and inclination.

(Please note: this recipe contains raw egg.)

1 large sweet Romaine lettuce
1 clove garlic
100g Parmesan cheese in a block
1 large sea bass fillet or more
2 large egg yolks
2 tbsp white wine vinegar
200ml olive oil, about 150ml regular and
50ml extra virgin for flavour
2 tbsp cream, yogurt or crème fraiche
Crispy bread croutons

1. Prepare the Romaine and wash it thoroughly, then spin it dry. Crush the garlic. Finely grate about a quarter of the cheese and shave the rest into flakes with a potato peeler.

2. Score the skin of the sea bass fillet to help even cooking. Heat a frying pan over a moderate heat, add 1 tbsp olive oil and then the fish fillet, skin side down. Cook for 2–3 minutes, then turn and cook for a further 2–3 minutes, depending on size, until just cooked.

3. Make the dressing while the bass is cooking. Place the egg yolks in a bowl, add the vinegar and garlic, and whisk lightly to combine. Trickle the oils into the bowl in a steady stream whilst whisking – this is easy and

it's really not worth having to wash up a blender. You are aiming for a sauce about the consistency of thick, unwhipped cream. Add a little salt and pepper, then the grated cheese and cream. Whisk again and add more seasoning to taste.

4. Tear the lettuce into generous pieces and toss it in a little of the dressing. Start layering it on plates. Flake the bass and snip the skin, if crispy, into shreds if you like to eat it. Add some fish, croutons and Parmesan flakes to the Romaine, spoon a little of the remaining dressing over and then repeat the layers. Caesar salad is pretty filling and rich, so don't make the portions too big, especially if you are serving it as a starter.

Tzatziki

Serves 4

I really do like cucumbers a lot and never tire of this popular Greek dip – and it's so much better when it is home-made.

1 tsp cumin seeds
½ cucumber, or more, skin on
2 cloves garlic
200–250g natural yogurt, thick Greek-style yogurt is best
Paprika, smoked if you wish
Freshly chopped mint, lemon or lime zest (optional)

1. Heat a small frying pan, add the cumin seeds, dry-fry for just a few seconds until fragrant, then turn into a mixing bowl. Coarsely grate the cucumber and squeeze dry in your hand or through a sieve. Crush the garlic into the bowl.

2. Mix all the ingredients together, adding a little paprika to the dip with good sea salt and pepper to taste, and sprinkling a little more over the top for colour. Serve with crusty bread or pittas, as part of a mixed mezze or as a sauce with barbecued meats.

Strawberries

May–October; glasshouse berries
March–April and November–December

A jewel of summer, with their shiny red skins embossed with almost unnoticeable seeds, strawberries are ubiquitous with both great society events and private parties, the perfect Pimm's and the perfect pick-me-up. Like tomatoes, they are at once accessible yet challenging – maybe this is their allure? A balance of sweetness and acidity which, when sun ripened to perfection, gives a big round flavour summing up summer, with British berries generally beating imported fruits hands down in the flavour stakes. West Sussex leads the way in getting British berries on to our plates.

Gardeners have manipulated climate for centuries and strawberry boards, to raise the berries as high as possible towards the sun, can be seen beneath the roof spans on several walls in the glasshouses at West Dean Gardens, the Victorian answer to a small, early crop. These days most of our outdoor strawberries are produced in very adaptable polytunnels. Close them up when the weather is inclement, or raise their skirts when the sun is out, like ill-prepared day trippers paddling at the seaside. If the weather is cold, a crop can be forced into fruit just by keeping a tunnel closed. One particular farm, just outside Chichester, is usually the first commercial producer in the country to get outdoor berries on to our supermarket shelves.

Always remove your strawberries from the fridge about an hour before serving so that flavour upon eating is unchecked by cold. Try them roughly chopped and sprinkled with grated lime zest, a spoonful or two of sugar and a little chopped fresh chilli, green or red. Leave for at least 10 minutes, stir and then amaze your taste buds by serving with chocolate brownies.

Plenty of farm shops and smallholders also grow strawberries in our most suitable of climates. The fashion for pick-your-own is waning but there are still farms where you can work in the fields yourself, which is perfect if, like me, you are a home-made strawberry ice cream addict. Wherever you shop, West Sussex berries can be on your list almost all of the year.

Strawberry Sauce for Salmon

Serves 4

If I have a signature dish, this might be it. It takes a bit of courage to give it a go but it is a great combination, and certainly one that will have your guests impressed by your culinary daring and creativity.

400g strawberries
3 tbsp white wine, orange juice or
undiluted orange squash
1 tbsp caster sugar
2 tsp tarragon or chervil leaves, freshly chopped
1 tsp white wine vinegar
Tarragon to garnish

1. Hull and roughly chop the strawberries. Heat them with the wine for about 1 minute, until the wine is bubbling and the strawberries have just lost their 'polished' look.
2. Add the tarragon or chervil, and sugar, then leave to cool.
3. Blend the sauce until smooth, then season to taste with a little salt, plenty of pepper and the vinegar, and a little more sugar if necessary.
4. Serve the sauce with hot or cold salmon, garnished with small sprigs of tarragon.

Strawberry Ice Cream

Serves 6–8

Just about the easiest of ice creams to make and one of the best! If you can use both West Sussex berries and cream it is bound to be heavenly.

400–500g strawberries
Juice of ½ a lemon
175g icing sugar
300ml double cream
Freshly ground black pepper

1. Hull the strawberries and chop them roughly. Blend until smooth with the lemon juice, sugar and cream (I say 300ml as the size of large pots keeps changing). Add black pepper – up to 1 tbsp is good, but you might start more cautiously with 1 tsp.

2. Turn the mixture into an ice cream maker and freeze-churn. Alternatively, spoon into a suitable container and freeze for around 4 hours, stirring once or twice to ensure even, smooth freezing. Serve immediately after churning, or try shaping into quenelles or scoops with 2 spoons, and hardening in the freezer on baking sheets lined with non-stick parchment. Store the hardened creams in a freezer box. This makes serving the ice cream much easier.

Sweetcorn

August–September

Tendersweet, bicolour, sun-spot, pericarps – all this is sweetcorn speak and common farming lingo in the sunny months of a West Sussex summer. On the coastal plain, with an almost uninterrupted sun high in the sky, the crowds heading to our beaches will pass through tall fields of corn, destined for our farm shop shelves, and those of supermarkets up and down the country.

Local sweetcorn is a local obsession with me. I cut the kernels away from the cobs with a sharp knife as soon as I buy the corn, and freeze them if I am not going to use them immediately, to preserve the maximum sweetness. I use the kernels in stir-fries, quick vegetable stews, salads, soups, and even in cornbreads and muffins. Of course, the whole cobs are delicious too, either boiled or barbecued in their leafy wrappers. Eat sweetcorn raw, and as freshly picked as possible, to reveal the sweetness of the crop – the only downside of this experience is the lack of gorgeous melting butter always associated with hot sweetcorn.

Our largest local commercial grower and industry leader, Barfoots of Botley, is getting two crops simultaneously from its sweetcorn. It uses all the waste from the plants and processing to feed its biodigester, very efficiently producing much-needed electricity for the National Grid as well as fabulous corn to eat.

How can you tell sweetcorn from maize in a field? The crop for human consumption has yellow, not red, tassels on the cobs and is usually planted in double rows rather than blocks. And it tastes a whole lot better too!

◇────────◦◗●◖◦────────◇

Sussex Succotash

Serves 4–6

This filling dish is great with ham, cold chicken, or simply with green salad and buttered bread. Use 500g frozen sweetcorn kernels when fresh UK cobs are not in season.

4 cobs sweetcorn
1 small onion
1 red pepper
1–2 cloves garlic
2–3 red chillies
1 tbsp oil and a knob of butter

250g frozen soya or edamame beans, or garden peas
Parsley, chopped, to garnish

1. Shuck the corn and then cut the kernels away from the husks with a very sharp knife. Finely dice the onion and pepper, and very finely chop the garlic and the chillies – remove the seeds from the chillies for a milder flavour.

2. Heat the oil and a knob of butter in a large pan, add the onion and cook for 6–8 minutes until softened but not browned – the longer that you cook it, the sweeter it will be. Add all the remaining ingredients and stir until the beans or peas have defrosted. Cook over a low heat for 4–5 minutes, until everything is tender. Season with salt and pepper if needed, then stir in more butter and plenty of chopped parsley before serving.

Sweetcorn and Vanilla Soup

Serves 4

An autumn delight and a deliciously unusual combination of flavours.

4 cobs of sweetcorn
1 red chilli
1 medium onion

1 vanilla pod
25g butter
500ml milk
Paprika to garnish

1. Prepare the ingredients. Cut the kernels from the sweetcorn cobs using a sharp knife – you will have about 500g. Seed and finely chop the chilli; finely chop the onion. Cut the vanilla pod along its length with a sharp knife, then scrape out and reserve the seeds.

2. Melt the butter in a large saucepan, add the onion and chilli, and cook slowly for about 10 minutes until soft but not browned. Add the sweetcorn, the vanilla seeds and pod and 500ml water. Bring to the boil, cover and simmer for 5–6 minutes. Cool slightly, discard the vanilla pod and remove a little of the corn for garnish, then add the milk to the soup and blend until smooth.

3. Reheat, season, then serve with the reserved corn and a sprinkling of paprika.

Tomatoes

March–October (glasshouse);
July–September (outdoor)

I cannot imagine my kitchen without tomatoes – a culinary essential and a key ingredient in every cuisine except traditional Chinese dishes. Whatever you want to cook, here in West Sussex you can be using flavour-packed local tomatoes for eight months of the year.

It is, of course, all down to glasshouse growing and our fabulous West Sussex sunshine. From bite-sized Cocktail fruits and Baby Plums, to the huge round Beef variety, in colours from orange to deep purple, you'll find tomatoes that will taste as good as they look. Our local growers have led the way with natural pest control, commercial bee pollination and green energy production for heating the glasshouses for the extended West Sussex season. They are vine tomato specialists, for as long as a tomato is on the vine – on the plant or in the pack – it will absorb nutrients and flavour. 'Vine ripened' is not a marketing gimmick and completely delivers on flavour.

Sunshine is essential for a good tomato flavour. Without it, you'll need to add salt, pepper and a little sugar to compensate for the lack of natural sun-induced sweetening. Adding olive oil and salt completely changes a tomato. Just take a few minutes to slice and season your toms, then add a little oil and leave for 5 minutes or so to encourage a wonderful feast of flavours. Everyone thinks basil with tomatoes but why not try thyme? Rosemary is wonderful too, especially with cooked tomatoes, as its strong musky yet slightly citrus taste draws an added depth of rich flavour from the fruit.

Look for West Sussex on supermarket labels and you will be buying from Eric Wall Ltd at Barnham, Jakes Nursery at Sidlesham or Humber VHB at Runcton. Nutbourne Nursery near Pulborough is much more visible to everyone seeking local tomatoes in farms shops and independent stores. Its distinctive dark-green boxes full of multi-coloured varieties stand out on the shelves and in displays. Tomatoes should never be refrigerated as it actually causes a breakdown in the cell structure. The ideal is 11–12°C and warmer is better than colder.

West Sussex Tomato Tabbouleh Salsa

Serves 4–6

This flavour-packed fusion recipe mixes many different culinary ideas into a substantial salad that is great for barbecues, with cold meats or as part of a salad buffet. All the vegetables are grown in West Sussex.

2 chillies
2–3 cloves garlic
1 red onion
500g tomatoes
1 red pepper
1 cucumber
250g cracked or bulgar wheat
Mint and flat-leaf parsley
1 lemon, zest and juice
Olive or rapeseed oil, to taste

1. Seed the chilies then finely chop them with the garlic. Finely chop the onion, and dice the tomatoes and pepper. Grate half the cucumber and finely dice the remainder. Mix together in a large bowl, season with salt and leave to stand for 15–20 minutes, to extract lots of juices from the salsa.

2. Meanwhile, cover the wheat in a pan with a knuckle's depth of boiling water, then simmer for 4–5 minutes, until almost all the water is absorbed. Leave for 10 minutes, then stir into the salsa while still warm with the lemon zest and juice. Leave to cool.

3. Finely chop good handfuls of mint and parsley, and add to the salad with oil to moisten and extra salt to taste.

Roasted Tomato Ketchup

Makes about 600ml – 1 vinegar bottle and a tasting pot

This is very different from commercial ketchup – it's a sad day if we run out of this at home. (Yes, cookery writers like ketchup too!)

2kg ripe tomatoes
1 large onion
150ml distilled malt vinegar
Juice of 1 lemon (about 50ml)
1 tsp celery salt
1 tsp mustard powder
1 tsp ground ginger
¼ tsp ground white pepper
½ tsp picante or smoked paprika
150g Demerara sugar

1. Preheat the oven to gas mark 7/220°C. Place the tomatoes in a single layer in a large roasting tin – use 2 tins if necessary. Roughly chop the onion, unpeeled, and tuck the pieces in amongst the tomatoes, then season lightly with salt and pepper. Cook for 45–60 minutes, until the fruits are soft and the skins have split and slightly blackened.

2. Carefully drain off the liquid in the pan – allow it to cool and use it as tomato stock. Purée the tomatoes and onion, either in a mouli or a liquidiser, and then sieve.

3. Pour the tomato pulp into a large saucepan and add all the remaining ingredients. Stir until the sugar is dissolved then bring to the boil and simmer for at least 10 minutes, until the ketchup is a good pouring consistency. Pour carefully into washed and rinsed jars that have been dried in a warm oven. Fill to within 1cm of the top of the bottle. Seal immediately with a vinegar-proof lid – empty malt vinegar bottles and lids are perfect.

4. Keep in the fridge once cold and use within 3 months. Sterilise in bottles or freeze the ketchup for longer storage.

Watercress

Year round

Whilst many people think of Hampshire as the home of UK watercress – they do even have a Watercress Line railway – we have our own traditional, family watercress growers here in West Sussex, at Hambrook, near Chichester.

Hairspring Watercress is situated on the northern side of the old main coastal road to Portsmouth, just across the hurly burly of the traffic from Bosham, where the clear waters of the watercress streams empty into the picturesque harbour. Traditional bunched watercress truly represents this beautiful county and I love it!

Traditional cress is dark green, large leaved and spicy with pepper, just the stuff that Edd Scales of Hairspring Watercress grows as a year round crop. At Hairspring the water is regularly tested and is as clean as clean can be – in fact, I never wash my cress from them as I am certain that my water can't be as pure as theirs, and each bunch is washed before and after packing. Now labelled organic and certified by the Soil Association, this is a local superfood, being particularly rich in iron.

The cress keeps well but, of course, it is best eaten as fresh as possible. To keep it perky put the stalks in water with a thin plastic bag over the leaves – don't wrap the stalks in plastic as they need to take up water to keep the cress fresh. If the cress goes limp, put the leaves into water for a short time and then, when refreshed, turn the bunch up the other way with the stalks back in the water.

Watercress is so much more than a garnish, as these favourite recipes prove.

Ewe's Milk Cheese and Watercress Salad with Quince Dressing

Serves 2–4

A lovely West Sussex way to serve a cheese course as a salad, rather than simply from a board with biscuits.

1 bunch Hairspring Watercress
50g walnut halves
100g membrillo or quince paste
1 tbsp sherry or white wine vinegar

75–100ml extra virgin olive oil
75g hard ewe's milk cheese – Sussex Duddleswell,
Lord of the Hundreds or Berkswell

1. Trim the watercress, then wash, spin and leave to dry if you choose. Chop up the membrillo into small pieces.

2. Heat a non-stick frying pan, add the walnut halves and stir-fry gently until crisp – do not let the nuts burn. Leave to cool.

3. Gently heat the membrillo in a pan with 1 tsp of the vinegar until softened. Transfer to a bowl and gradually whisk or beat until smooth, then whisk in about half the olive oil. Add the remaining vinegar, season with salt and pepper, and then continue adding olive oil until the dressing has a thick spooning consistency.

4. Toss the cress in a little of the dressing then arrange it on a platter. Trim away the rind from the cheese and dice the curd. Scatter the cheese and walnuts over the cress, then spoon the dressing onto the salad. Serve immediately.

Creamy Pork, Leek and Walnut Stir-Fry

Serves 3–4

This meal-in-one is seasoned with watercress. Finely chopped and added at the last moment, it brings the dish to life. A perfect recipe to make with wet walnuts in season in the early autumn, or you could use cobnuts if you wish.

2 leeks
2 carrots
Bunch of watercress
400g can flageolet beans
300g pork stir-fry strips
½ tsp smoked paprika or pimentón
2 tbsp olive oil
50g walnut halves
150ml double cream
Chopped walnuts and paprika to garnish

1. Trim and rinse the leeks, then cut into ½cm slices. Cut the peeled carrots into 6mm batons. Trim and finely chop the watercress. Drain and rinse the beans. Dust the pork with the paprika.

2. Heat a wok over a high heat, add the oil then the pork and cook quickly until starting to brown. Add the leeks and carrots, and continue cooking for 3–4 minutes, until the vegetables are beginning to soften, then add the walnuts and cook for a further minute.

3. Stir the cream into the wok and add the beans, bring to the boil and cook for 2–3 minutes, until the beans are heated through. Add the watercress, then season to taste. Garnish with chopped walnuts and paprika, and serve with crusty bread.

Foraged
Foods

Blackberries

September–October

Are these oft-times sharp, bobbly little berries the ultimate foraged food? They are certainly the one that most people know about and, being borne abundantly on what is primarily a weed on wild ground or in the hedgerows, blackberries are one free food that is easily available to everyone.

The first hint of autumn brings out carrier bags, plastic pots and even upturned sun hats for ill-equipped foragers. Whilst brambles by roads and railways, lanes and seashores offer fruit for those who do not venture off-road, the berries that I seek out are the furthest away from traffic fumes, on footpaths and in hedgerows. With 2,831 km (1,759 miles) of public footpaths and 1,173 km (729 miles) of public bridleways in West Sussex there are certainly lots of non-tainted brambling opportunities for us.

Some of the most easily accessible berries that I have found have been on footpaths in nature reserves, where the brambles are cut back every year, keeping the stems vigorous in fruiting at pickable heights. One year we found trusses of berries like prolific baby tomatoes dripping from the hedgerows in a coastal reserve. Obviously the birds like the berries too, but there are always plenty for them and us.

For jam and jelly making you want your berries to be underripe rather than over – the preserve will keep better made with berries that show no signs of deterioration. Such berries will, however, be a little sharper than truly ripe ones, which are best for pies, crumbles, compotes and ice creams. Inevitably we tend to marry blackberries to apples but they are also delicious with pears, and when used to add a tiny seasoning of sweetness to seasonal savoury dishes. Blackberries also freeze really well. We have some friends who pick enough berries each autumn to have on their muesli everyday throughout the year. Just open-freeze them on baking trays, then crumble them up into individual berries and pack them into bags or boxes once solid. This keeps them separate during storage so that you can remove just as many as you want, as and when.

Bramble Jelly

Makes about 5 x 500g jars

This was my favourite jam in childhood and it's still a strong contender now. I think it's the real taste of the countryside in autumn.

2kg blackberries
2 large lemons
500ml water
Granulated sugar

1. Pick over the blackberries and discard any squashy ones, then place the berries in a large pan. Grate the zest from the lemons into the pan and squeeze the juice. Add this to the pan with the measured water. Simmer, covered, for 40 minutes or so, until the fruit is very soft.

2. Set up a jelly bag on a stand and spoon the fruit into the bag. Leave it to drain – this will take several hours and I usually leave it for 4 hours or overnight. Chill a saucer in the fridge.

3. Thoroughly wash and rinse some jars in hot water and set them, upside down, on the wire shelves in a cool oven (gas mark 3/160°C, or the simmering oven of an Aga) to dry whilst completing the jelly.

4. Squeeze the last drops of liquid from the bag – the jelly is so dark in colour that it will not matter if it goes slightly cloudy. Measure the extract into a preserving

pan adding 450g sugar to every 500ml. Heat, stirring until the sugar has dissolved, then boil rapidly until a gel starts to form on a wooden spoon dipped into the pan. When a gel forms on the spoon drop a little onto the chilled saucer – if it sets in a few seconds and wrinkles when pushed with your fingertip, the jelly is ready.

5. Pour into the hot dry jars, cover and seal. Label when cool and store in a cool, dark place.

Venison Sausages with Apples, Blackberries and Pumpkin

Serves 2–3

All-in-one meals mean less washing up! This simple recipe can easily be cooked by or with children.

1 medium leek
1 small wedge of pumpkin, about 200g
1 large Bramley apple
1 tbsp oil
6 thick venison sausages

150ml dry cider or apple juice
1 bay leaf
1 large handful or so of blackberries

1. Trim and slice the leek; peel and seed the pumpkin and cut into 1½cm dice; and peel, core and slice the apple.
2. Heat a large frying pan and add the oil. Brown the sausages thoroughly on all sides then add the prepared fruit and vegetables and cook for 3–4 minutes. Add the cider or apple juice with the bay leaf and simmer for about 15 minutes until the sausages are cooked. Add more cider or apple juice as and when necessary.
3. Add the blackberries and heat them briefly, then season to taste with salt, pepper and sugar before serving.

Elderflowers and Elderberries

May (flowers); September (berries)

Elder trees grow prolifically in West Sussex. They are in our churchyards, on wasteland and on the Downs – they are well suited to chalk but, like most plants, prefer well-fertilised soils, so are also often found on field margins and are in many hedgerows. With the replanting of native hedging species across the county there are more elders, and therefore plenty of delicious elderflowers and berries to forage. The flowers are easy to use but the berries must always be cooked. Oh! The agonies and frustration of train journeys in May revealing trees laden with flowers on inaccessible land!

Walking through West Sussex is the best indication that the elderflowers are ready for collection: the scent of the tree is sensational. Indeed, I think if you can't smell the flowers you shouldn't collect them: the scent is nature at work, luring us to harvest at a moment of perfect ripeness. Pick elderflowers in the morning on a still, warm day and please resist the temptation to wash them before use – you will wash away much of the flavour. If the selected tree is accessible from all sides you will find several days, if not weeks, pass before the flowers are ready on the northern side as opposed to the sun-drenched south side. This is really useful for cordial production: there are only so many boxes or bowls of steeping liquors that any fridge can accommodate at one time! With so many elder trees to choose from it is much better to walk a little way from the road, to gather flowers that are not coated in traffic fumes.

The uses of elderflowers and their cordial are well documented but the berries are less widely exploited, an oversight as they provide an excellent winter tonic. They must be cooked – both the leaves and raw berries are poisonous. That said, they have an almost tannic fruity flavour and so the most common use of elderberries is in fruit vinegars, mixed jams and in game dishes, where they might be added to a gravy or jus in a frying or roasting pan.

Elderberry Refresher

Makes about 1 litre

I love this, diluted to taste with either hot or cold water, or tonic. It is slightly spicy and almost like red grape juice. Add it neat to pan juices when cooking game or poultry. Allspice is not mixed spice; also called Jamaican pepper, it is a pungent yet aromatic seasoning.

500g ripe plump elderberries
1 lemon
750ml water
¼ tsp ground allspice
500g granulated sugar
25g tartaric acid

1. Snip away any thick stalks from the elderberries. Grate the zest from the lemons and squeeze the juice.
2. Cook the fruit with the lemon zest and juice in the water with the allspice. Bring to the boil then simmer, covered, for 30 minutes or until the berries have softened and started to burst.
3. Strain through a jelly bag or a muslin-lined sieve. Add the sugar and tartaric acid and boil until reduced to a slightly syrupy consistency. Pour into warm bottles, or cool completely and pour into a clean dry milk container. Seal and keep refrigerated. This should keep for about 2–3 months – but I bet you drink it before

then, diluted with tonic or sparkling water. Freeze for longer storage.

Elderflower Cordial

Makes 2 litres (3½ pints) cordial

This is Katie Stewart's recipe (printed with her permission) for one of the best flavours of early summer. Katie was adamant that the elderflowers must be picked on a dry, sunny day. I have changed the recipe, adding tartaric acid instead of citric, on the advice of a home-brew expert who suggested that it gave a fuller flavour. It does, tartaric acid being from grapes. I think Kate would have liked it my way.

If you cannot get citric or tartaric acid, use 5 lemons instead of 2 and increase the acid that way. It helps to stop any fermentation on prolonged storage – mind you, this is so delicious I cannot see that being a problem!

Choose a dry sunny morning then pick newly opened elderflower heads that are creamy coloured for maximum flavour. Drop them gently into a large polythene bag. Get them home and make the cordial soon as you can – the recipe is simple.

30 elderflower heads
2 lemons, scrubbed and sliced

1 x 50g pack citric acid
1.8kg granulated sugar

1. Turn the elderflowers gently onto the kitchen draining board or a table top and any tiny insects will scuttle out. Snip the main stalk from each elderflower head and let the flowers drop into a large mixing bowl.

2. Add the sliced lemons, citric acid and the granulated sugar. Bring 1½ litres cold water to the boil and pour over the mixture. Stir to dissolve the sugar, then cover the bowl and leave the mixture for 5 days – stirring it once a day (I usually keep it in the fridge at this stage).

3. Line a colander with double-thickness butter muslin and set over a mixing bowl. Scald the muslin by pouring through boiling water from a kettle, then discard the water in the bowl underneath. Turn the elderflower brew – flowers, lemon slices and liquid – into the muslin-lined colander and let the cordial strain through. Discard everything left behind in the colander (or use a jelly bag).

4. I bottle my cordial in 2 x 1 litre bottles – could be lemonade or mineral water bottles, or some of the stylish glass bottles you can find in hardware stores. Use a jug to scoop the cordial from the bowl and pour into the bottles of your choice.

5. Your cordial will keep in the refrigerator for up to 3 months. If, as I do, you want your cordial to last longer (from one season to the next) the answer is to introduce a Campden tablet – a preservative used by home

winemakers and usually available from a chemist. Simply crush 1 Campden tablet to a powder and mix with 1 tbsp cold water to dissolve it. Add the solution to the cordial after straining but before pouring into the bottles and your cordial will keep for up to 1 year.

6. To serve: pour about 2–3 tablespoons into a tumbler. Add ice and a slice of lemon and fill up with tonic water (my preference) or sparkling mineral water – the fizz is refreshing.

Katie Stewart

When Katie Stewart died in January 2013, West Sussex lost its most influential, unassuming and talented food writer. Kate was a legend, an inspiration and a friend.

Kate was of the old school, she knew her stuff and all the technical reasons why things happen in the kitchen. Her columns in *The Times* and *Woman's Journal* inspired generations and her later work in the BBC's *Homes & Antiques* magazine was welcomed by her many fans.

A proud Scot, Kate spent a number of years in Kent, and settled in Cuckfield for the later part of her career and her retirement. Some of her relatives were fruit growers – we spoke once about the difference in flavour between wild and cultivated blackberries. She said her family had been involved at the very beginning of growing them commercially but that it hadn't worked well, despite the sweet flavour and thornless stems – she said she thought people wouldn't pay for something they could pick for free, if only they could be bothered. She gave me her elderflower cordial recipe to use – when you know about and love food as Kate did, sharing is just the natural thing to do.

We first met when she gave a fundraising demonstration for the Weald & Downland Open Air Museum in Chichester. Kate came to Arundel to open my deli in 1988. There were queues of people to see her, clutching their copies of *The Times Cookery Book*, or *Katie Stewart's Cookbook* in various states of splatter and dog-earedness, hoping for a smile, a chat and a signature. She disappointed no one. She was iconic for our generation and my cousin Andy, a chemical engineer who learnt to cook for survival, came down from Lichfield in Staffordshire, not only to support his little cousin but to get his thumbed and much-loved *Times Cookery Book* signed.

In my years editing the *Seasons* magazine for Waitrose, it was to Kate who I turned to for a contribution to the very first issue. I remember giving away copies at the *Country Living* Christmas Fair in Islington and the delight when recipients found Kate's recipes – she was an inspiration to so many.

In later years Kate came to talk to our Transition Chichester food group about bottling, one of the many subjects that she knew so much about. Held in the fabulous Tudor Room in the Bishop's Palace, Kate arrived to find the then Bishop of Chichester and his wife hugely excited about her visit and armed with their copies of her much-used books, ready for her to sign! She gave many demonstrations to raise funds for local charities. She loved farmers' markets and the growing appetite for local food. She was particularly interested in the local cheeses from Sussex High Weald Dairy, which was close to her home.

I contributed to BBC Radio 4's *Last Word* tribute to Kate and it was broadcast on the day of her funeral – I heard it on the way home. She had been Mayor of Cuckfield and very much a part of village life. She is much missed but her glorious writing lives on.

Kate's top tip? Put a spoonful of flour under your joint before roasting – it starts the gravy off and stops it being lumpy.

Juniper

August–September

Juniper used to be common throughout the UK but loss of habitat has resulted in the bushes on the chalklands of the south of England becoming increasingly important, although they are not commercial. With the growth in popularity of 'designer gins' we certainly need juniper, the major flavouring of this very British spirit, to flourish and it does grow happily in West Sussex on the more open areas of woodland on the Downs.

Juniper, as I know it in West Sussex, is a small, hardy tree or shrub, sometimes reaching 100 years of age or more, and is often found near yew trees. Of course, there are many varieties and several produce berries, but the juniper of the Downs needs an 18-month cycle to produce usable spice fruits. In the first year the berries are green and, like unbrined olives, are of no use at all. They must be left on the bush for another season, through to the following late summer or autumn, to ripen and blacken, ready for using fresh or being dried. The traditional use of juniper is to make sauces for autumnal game: pheasant, partridge, rabbit and venison – as well, of course, as an aromatic for gin.

A word of caution if you do look for juniper up on the Downs: as it grows near yew trees, please ensure that you are not on a nature reserve with your secateurs primed – unless you have checked the reserve noticeboard for harvesting/foraging permissions.

◦———◦•◦———◦

Partridge with Gin, Orange and Juniper

Serves 4

Choose a roasting tin large enough to take the birds with space around them, otherwise they will steam and not roast. This is important for all foods being roasted. Partridge is eaten slightly pink, but you can cook them for about 40 minutes if you like them more well done. Much depends on your preference and the size and age of the birds. Bread sauce is good with this too.

1 large onion
4 rashers streaky bacon
2 tsp juniper berries
2 bay leaves

2 oranges
1 tbsp flour
4 young partridge
2 tbsp olive oil
Fresh parsley
100ml gin

1. Preheat the oven to gas mark 7/220°C. Finely slice the onion, stretch the bacon rashers and cut them in half, and crush the juniper, either in a pestle and mortar or with the back of a spoon. Grate the zest from the oranges and squeeze the juice.

2. Place the onion with the juniper, bay leaves, orange zest and flour in the bottom of a roasting tin large enough to take the birds with room around them, then sit the partridge on top. Season the birds with salt and pepper, then place a piece of bacon on each breast. Drizzle the oil over the birds, then roast them in the hot oven for 20 minutes.

3. Remove the bacon from the partridge and roast for a further 10 minutes, until golden. Meanwhile, chop and reserve the bacon rashers, and wash and chop lots of parsley for garnish.

4. Remove the partridge from the pan and allow them to rest for at least 10 minutes, but keep them warm by covering them with a tent of foil. Return the bacon to the pan and stir all the ingredients over a medium heat on the hob. Add the gin – it probably will not flame because of everything else in the pan, but be prepared to pull it

off the heat, just in case it does. Add the orange juice, then bring the sauce to the boil, stirring all the time. It will make a thin pouring sauce. Remove the bay leaves.

5. Season the sauce to taste using salt, pepper and a little sugar if necessary. Stir in most of the parsley.

6. Serve the partridge whole, with the sauce spooned over and garnished with more parsley.

Juniper and Walnut Bread Sauce

Serves 4

This is excellent with all game birds, and with chicken and turkey. A modern twist on a very traditional recipe. Breads differ enormously – you might need to add a little more, or a little more milk, according to your preference for saucy thickness.

1 tsp juniper berries
250ml milk
1 bay leaf
1 thick slice white bread, weighing about 100 g
Butter
50g walnut pieces

1. Crush the juniper berries lightly, then heat them in a pan with the milk and the bay leaf until almost boiling. Remove from the heat, cover and leave to infuse for 10 minutes. Strain the flavourings from the milk. Rinse the pan and return the milk to it (rinsing is important to stop the milk catching on the base of the pan when you reheat it).

2. Break the bread into small pieces – I leave the crust on but you can remove it if you wish. Stir into the milk with a generous knob of butter and leave to soften for 10 minutes. Beat the mixture until smooth with a wooden spoon. Add a little more milk if it is too thick. Roughly chop the walnuts.

3. Heat the sauce again when required and season with salt and pepper. Stir in the walnut pieces just before serving.

Sea Vegetables

There is a real and growing interest in seaweeds and sea vegetables, not only for the fun of foraging for them but also as they are true superfoods, rich in vitamins and minerals which promote good health. The important thing is to know the quality of the seawater in your chosen area of harvest, or the use of the area for dog walks. A good starting point is to check the EC Blue Flag awards for local beaches and to start your foraging for sea vegetables there (Littlehampton, Bognor Regis and West Wittering all held Blue Flags in 2013).

The most common sea vegetable in use at the moment is samphire. Crisp and bright green with a salty tang, we became aware of it in restaurants and on fishmongers slabs as a partner or garnish for sea trout in the summer months. Marsh samphire, the best variety, has a very short season in late June and July, and is at its best when tender. Rock samphire grows above the waterline and needs to be cooked before being eaten.

The succulent oval leaves of sea purslane have a slightly silvery sheen which helps them to withstand the weather on the salt marshes where it is found. Straggling across large areas it is perhaps the easiest of the sea veg to pick, but it needs quite a long cook to tenderise it, especially if you pick in the winter months. It looks a bit like sage, and goes well in grain and rice dishes.

My favourite of all sea vegetables, both to look at and for a wonderful early vegetable crop, is sea kale. I grow it in my gravel garden, conditions which it loves, and force the crowns as they appear to give tender white spears, a delicacy long before West Sussex asparagus is ready. Sea kale forcers are squatter and more bell shaped than those for rhubarb, which are taller and thinner. The kale grows profusely on our pebbly beaches. The grey, crinkly leaves are architecturally of such interest that it is often used in gardens as a border plant, and they look wonderful on our beaches all year round. Sea kale thongs are available through many plant companies.

Steamed Sea Kale with Halloumi

This is hardly a recipe, but is so delicious that anyone living near the beach might like to try it.

Tender white sea kale stems
Butter
Black pepper or freshly grated nutmeg
Griddled halloumi cheese
Hot buttered toast to serve

1. Trim the kale and wash it well if you have collected it from the beach. Cut any thicker stems in half vertically for even cooking.

2. Place in a colander over a pan of boiling water and cover with the saucepan lid. Steam for 4–5 minutes, then pierce with the tip of a sharp knife to check for tenderness. When cooked it should still have a bit of a bite to it.

3. Meanwhile, slice and fry the halloumi in a little butter, and toast one slice of bread per person. Butter the toast, add some of the halloumi, and pile the sea kale on top of it with a knob of butter and a little pepper or nutmeg (both are lovely). Top with the remaining cheese and serve.

Samphire Salad with Selsey Crab

Serves 4 as a starter or 2 as a main

Use finely shredded fennel or crisp Iceberg, Romaine or Sweet Gem lettuce for this wonderful salad with lemon and crab.

2 handfuls of tender marsh samphire
1 lemon
Olive oil
2 hand-picked Selsey crabs
Lettuce or fennel

1. Pick over the samphire, removing any woody pieces and wash it well. Shake or spin it dry.

2. Finely chop a whole lemon, pith and flesh and remove any seeds. Sprinkle with a little sea salt and leave for 5 minutes. Add 3 tbsp olive oil and stir, then add a little more oil to make a dressing of spoonable consistency. Season to taste, but be light with the salt because of the samphire.

3. Mix the samphire with shredded lettuce or fennel, then toss with half the lemon dressing and pile on to plates. Top with the crab meat and serve with the remaining dressing spooned over.

Wild Garlic

March–April

Winter seems to drag on. Sometimes even the garden rhubarb doesn't want to brave the cold and the 'hungry months' appear interminable. Then you are out in the countryside – or sometimes even in an undisturbed area in town – and come across a sunny bank or a slope in a woodland bare of leaves, and there is a wonderful aroma of something that you know so well from the kitchen. Where is it? What is it? Bright green lanky leaves filling out and darkening to an almost tulip-like appearance as the scent increases, well before the white starburst flowers are held high on a triangular stalk. It's wild garlic time, so spring is on its way!

One of the delights of wild garlic – or ransoms, to give the traditional name – is that the leaves, stalk and flower heads of the plant can all be used. The leaves emerge first and then countless kitchens burst into pesto-making mode and suddenly there's a touch of the Med creeping into the cuisine again, even for the most dedicated of local, seasonal cooks. I often use walnuts in my West Sussex wild garlic pesto, with local rapeseed oil and Bookhams Parmesan-style cheese.

Red Lentil Dhal with Wild Garlic

Serves 4

This is a top favourite no-meat meal. The dhal itself is very satisfying, and even better if you fry some extra onions and mix them with freshly chopped chilli for a garnish. I really like to serve it with a seasonal vegetable rice. I chop or shred a mixture of veg very finely, almost to chef-like fineness, and add to basmati rice just before it is cooked. Give a quick stir, cook for 2 minutes, then leave covered to steam, off the heat, for 5 minutes or so. A really satisfying meal.

250g red lentils
1 onion, finely chopped
4 green cardamoms
2 tbsp oil 4–6 cloves
1 tsp cumin seeds
Handful of wild garlic leaves
Fried onions and freshly chopped chilli
to garnish (optional)

1. Wash the lentils in a sieve and shake dry. Finely chop the onion and crush the cardamom pods lightly.

2. Heat a pan, add the oil with the cardamom, cloves and cumin and cook for a few seconds until fragrant, then add the onion. Cook, covered, over a low heat for 5 minutes, until the onion is softened.

3. Add the lentils with sufficient water to cover them by about 1cm. Bring to the boil, then cover and simmer for 15–20 minutes, until the lentils are tender, beating frequently to make them creamy. Add a little more water during cooking if necessary.

4. Wash the garlic leaves and shred them finely. Beat the lentils again, add the garlic, then season to taste with salt and pepper. Serve with curries, or as suggested above, simply with freshly cooked rice and vegetables in season, and with onions and chilli garnish if you wish.

⊰•◦•⊱

Trout with Wild Garlic and Buttered Cucumber

Serves 2

Ransoms, or wild garlic, is the most obliging of free foods. Its delicate scent ensures that you are picking the right thing and it is wonderful with fish.

2 small trout, about 250g each
½ a cucumber, or more
A large handful of wild garlic, leaves plus a
few stalks and flowers
2 tbsp oil, e.g. olive or rapeseed
Butter

1. Remove the fins of the trout and the heads if you wish. Dice a good chunk of cucumber and chop the wild garlic – leaves, stalks and flowers – reserving 2 of the leaves whole.

2. Wrap one broad leaf of garlic around each fish, tucking the stalk into the belly cavity with a little chopped flower stalks and heads.

3. Melt a good knob of butter with the oil in a large preheated frying pan, add the trout with the neatest leaf side down and fry quickly for 2 minutes, then reduce the heat and continue cooking for 2–3 minutes. Turn and brown the other side of the fish, then cook for 2 minutes. Add the cucumber with more chopped garlic leaves, stalks and flowers, and cook just for 1 minute or so, turning in the buttery juices. This is lovely with new potatoes and peppery, leafy salad.

Wild Plums

July–August

From yellow to deep-cherry red and damson-like purple, wild plums or bullaces are common in hedgerows and are more than reward for the antics needed to harvest them. Not much larger than dessert cherries, these fruits have to be really ripe to be good. For fruit gin, my favourite use, they should be as ripe and therefore as sweet as possible.

To spot your wild plums you'll have to look down or up! Down, as they will fall easily and the stones will litter the pathway if the birds are feasting before you are. Up, and on smallish trees, a bit like elder, and which you should have noticed earlier in the year covered in plum-like blossom, you will spot green fruits changing colour in the sun as they ripen. Keep an eye out and your Christmas drinks selection will be greatly added to with some homemade plum gin. Take a stick with you for pulling down the branches to make picking the fruit easier, but don't break them or you will not be able to reach the fruit at all next year.

As the plums are quite small it is much like pitting cherries if you want to cook with them, but the reward is that they make a great sauce with duckling, and are good with pork, pigeon and Chinese-style lamb casseroles or stir-fries. You may well need to add sugar with your seasonings.

When I have made and bottled my gin there is the annual dilemma of what to do with the alcohol pickled fruit. I can never bring myself to throw it away and so a few spoonfuls of the plums go into spiced pork casseroles and stir-fries, meat loaves and sweet fruit crumbles. There are always more stones than fruit but the flavour is unmissable, if mainly gin! I keep the fruit in a covered plastic pot in the fridge until it is all used up.

Wild Plum Gin

Makes about 1½ litres

You can also use this recipe for sloe gin, sloes being plentiful in most hedgerows most years. Both are good but the plums have a much more fruity flavour.

1kg wild plums
1kg granulated sugar
1 litre gin

1. Wash the plums then prick them all over, or put them in a strong carrier bag and roll them firmly with a rolling pin to break the skins. Turn into a bowl or lidded plastic box, and add the sugar and gin. Stir to get the sugar dissolving, then cover and leave somewhere cool – I always put it in the fridge if the room temperature is above 20°C. Keep the gin bottle for later.

2. Stir every day for a week to ensure that the sugar has dissolved, then leave for a month.

3. Strain the gin then pour it into the reserved, clean bottle plus an extra jar too, or use a decanter if you have one. Keep until Christmas to mature before using. A splash in the bottom of a glass of cheap fizz is always good!

Growing
Communities

The one thing that really changed my whole approach to cooking was ordering a veg box. Paying out each week for fruit and veg made me think about what to cook according to the longevity of the produce in the pack. It was a creatively liberating experience for my culinary skills. Many schemes are available in West Sussex, with Riverford having their own farm at Worthing for the local market, but it is the small local market gardeners that I encourage you to support if you don't grow your own and would like a produce box from some people who do.

I live in Chichester and there are three veg schemes close to me: Veg Out at Sidlesham, Wayside Organics at Oving and Tuppenny Barn at Southbourne, near Emsworth. There are great stories about each of them. For example, Wayside have a weekly round as well as supplying the new macro village shop in their local pub, The Gribble Inn (which also brews its own beer). You can see a local food community taking shape!

Maggie Haynes at Tuppenny Barn sells mainly through her own mini-shop on the A259. She has established an eco-friendly education centre on her 2½ acre plot to accommodate the growing number of groups that wish to visit the site, either to learn about fruits and vegetables, or to volunteer some time and muscle and get their hands dirty. Maggie is ex-army, a Northern Ireland military veteran, and this site has much more order about it than the most organic schemes, which are inevitably hard work.

These produce suppliers really fill the void between grow-your-own and supermarket supplies, but there are also an increasing number of community growing projects across the county, similar to ours in my home village of Tangmere. We garden as a group on an area of land loaned to us by the parish council. Around 30 adults take a share of the work and a share of the produce, and we have about a dozen children who come along regularly as well. Crop heroes have emerged, taking responsibility for getting the chosen crops into the ground, and for successional sowings of everything that needs more than one hit. Shared meals and coffee breaks are as important as gardening, and we were inspired in our early days by the work of Kate Brickell and her team of adults with learning difficulties on their community garden at Petworth. Our lovely Friends of the Community Garden support our fundraising open days and cookery demonstrations, and our livestock – chickens and pigs – delight all who walk past.

There is research to show that time-poor gardeners who abandon their allotments will look instead to local growers to supply their produce. However you want to achieve local fruit and veg, West Sussex has an offer that will suit you perfectly.

Dairy
& Eggs

Butter

I'm a butter girl – I love it: good butter, butter that is just made with good salt and not mixed with oil to make it spread easily from the fridge or anything like that. A block of creamy yellow butter. If I cannot have that on my bread I don't want anything else.

Good butter is still made by small dairies and usually by cheesemakers who diversify into it as a sideline to increase their product range. West Sussex-made butter comes from one of our cheesemakers, who stores the cream for 3 days before churning it into butter, allowing a rich flavour to develop. Larger cheesemakers might skim fat from whey, the thin liquid left after cheesemaking, to utilise any last fat molecules in that to make a cooking butter, which is particularly suitable for savoury foods. Butter made by a small producer has fabulous flavour: it is an artisan product.

The most famous use of butter in West Sussex is for pond pudding, a staple of centuries past when a more active lifestyle allowed for such buttery treats. I have also found it referred to as 'Sussex well pudding'. The pond is thought to be a reference to hammer ponds, relics now but then an essential part of the Tudor and Stuart-age iron industry in the Weald of Kent and Sussex. Streams and rivers were damned to make ponds, originally to cool the iron and then to drive waterwheels to power furnace bellows.

Most recipes suggest that the pudding should be a suet crust with a buttery filling, which spills out when the pudding is cut. I have tweaked that – suet and butter in one dish? Not these days! The lemon is a talking point; spoon out the cooked centre if you like a really lemony tang to your pudding.

West Sussex Pond Pudding

Serves 4

It has taken me close to 60 years to make a pond pudding. How I regret that now! I hope that this delicious recipe revives a county curiosity as it deserves to be a winter favourite. Of course it must be made with South Downs butter.

200g butter
200g self-raising flour
1 lemon
125g caster sugar
½–1 tsp mixed spice
100g currants

1. Freeze the butter for at least 2 hours then grate it coarsely just before use. Butter a 600–750ml pudding basin with the butter paper, then reserve the paper for cooking.

2. Grate the lemon zest into the flour in a bowl and add 25g sugar and half the butter. Stir then mix to a soft, manageable dough with cold water. Knead lightly on a floured surface and roll out to a circle a little under 1cm thick. Cut one third of the dough out in a segment and reserve it, then press the remainder into the pudding basin and shape it to fit right up to the rim with your gently rounded fist.

3. Mix the remaining butter, sugar, spice and currants. Prick the lemon all over with a fork and trim the pointy end off if necessary. Spoon some of the sugar mix into the basin, then add the lemon and spoon the remainder of the buttery sugar over. It will fill the basin well.

4. Reshape the reserved dough into a round and roll out to fit the top of the basin. Damp the edges of the dough in the basin with cold water as well as the edge of the underside of the lid. Top the pudding with the lid, seal the dampened edges together and crimp them closed by

pressing the edges of the dough together between the first finger of one hand and the first finger and thumb of your other hand, right around the basin.

5. Place the reserved butter paper on a generous sheet of foil, then fold them together across the centre to make a pleat – this allows the pudding to rise during cooking. Cover the basin with the foil lid, with the butter paper inside to stop the pud sticking to the foil. Tie the foil round the basin securely with string, using the rim of the basin to anchor it tightly.

6. Place the pudding on a metal trivet or an upturned old saucer in the bottom of a deep saucepan. Fill with hot water to halfway up the basin, then bring to the boil and simmer for 2½–3 hours, with the pan covered. Check it once or twice and add more water to the pan if necessary.

7. Lift the basin carefully from the pan with your hands well protected by a dry cloth (wet cloths are no barrier to heat and in fact magnify it). Remove the foil cover, loosen the edges of the pudding with a palette knife then invert the pud onto a dished serving plate (to catch the 'pond' juices) and shake firmly to release the pudding. Cut at the table and serve with whatever you dare: cream, ice cream, golden syrup or a promise to diet tomorrow...

Cheese

The craft of artisan cheesemaking is ever expanding throughout the UK. With around 900 entries each year to the British Cheese Awards, it is my hope that we shall soon be seeing more of our own cheesemakers scooping medals at these prestigious awards. We can create a cheeseboard of cow, sheep and goat's milk cheeses, including softs and blues, from our home terroir – and these cheeses are very good indeed.

Artisan cheese is all about flavour. They might not all be big and immediate on the palate but the flavour of a well-made, hand-crafted cheese develops in the mouth as the cheese warms, and releases hints of the quality of the milk and the skill of the cheesemaker. Although I generally prefer stronger flavours I am completely seduced by the creamy acidity of Sussex Slipcote soft cheeses, made with ewe's milk. All varieties are completely delicious in salads, sliced and grilled on top of risottos, or stirred into hot pasta. These are made by High Weald Dairy, which also produces the hard, tangy and pungently sweet Duddleswell, which is marvellous shaved over deli meats, Caesar salads and pizzas, as well as with watercress.

We do have our very own pasta cheese, a Parmesan-alike, made near Rudgwick by Bookhams. Bookhams also makes Sussex Charmer, a hybrid of its pasta cheese and Cheddar, which is very strong and marvellous for all gratins and bakes with cheese toppings. Low-fat cheeses are so often low on flavour. It is much better to use a small amount of a cheese like Charmer and get some flavour.

I have always enjoyed blue cheeses and am a fan of Molecombe Blue, one of the growing number of cheeses being produced at Goodwood Home Farm. It is soft and blue-veined: creamy, sharp and as good in salads and antipasti as it is on a cheeseboard.

Broccoli with Molecombe Blue and Chillies

The quantities for this delicious warm salad starter depend on your appetite. The recipe was inspired by Andy Stephenson, chef – patron of Hallidays of Funtington – a family restaurant that really does local, seasonal food brilliantly.

Purple sprouting broccoli, young, tender shoots
Garlic
Red chillies
Nuts of your choice (cobnuts, walnuts and less local pine nuts all work well)
Molecombe Blue cheese
Extra virgin olive oil

1. Trim the broccoli and split any slightly thicker stalks. Finely chop some garlic and red chilli, and roughly chop some nuts. Fork some cheese into small rough pieces.

2. Steam the broccoli until just tender. At the same time, heat a small frying pan, add a little oil, then add the garlic and chilli, off the heat. Cook gently for 1–2 minutes without browning, then add the nuts and remove from the heat.

3. Arrange the broccoli on individual plates and add the cheese. Top with the chilli, garlic and nut mix, a little salt and pepper, and drizzle with olive oil before serving.

Pasta with Spinach and Goat's Cheese

Serves 4

This is wonderful made with Sussex Slipcote – I think the pepper variety is my favourite.

1 large red pepper
300g dried pasta of your choice
250g prepared leaf spinach
Knob of butter
100g Sussex Slipcote
Freshly grated nutmeg

1. Quarter, seed then finely slice the pepper. Roughly shred the prepared spinach.

2. Cook the pasta in boiling, salted water as directed on the packet.

3. Place the spinach in a colander and set it over the pasta in the pan while it is cooking – place the saucepan lid over the spinach and steam for 2 minutes (the base of the colander may be in the pasta water, but that is OK). Remove the colander and chop the spinach in it with a metal spoon over the sink, until all the water has drained away and the spinach is finely chopped. Set aside on a plate.

4. Add the pepper to the pasta for the last 2 minutes of the cooking time. Drain the pasta and peppers in the colander.

5. Melt the butter with the cheese in the saucepan, then add the pasta, peppers and spinach, and toss them together in the cheese. Season well, and grate a little nutmeg over the pasta before serving.

Cream and
Ice Cream

Gastronomy or gluttony? Whatever it is that lures us to indulge in cream or ice cream, they are quintessential seaside ingredients and experiences. As a famous seaside county, West Sussex naturally has an appetite for them. No visit to the beach is really complete without a dairy delight but for too long all our ice creams were imported from across the borders, leaving no stamp of county-based provenance on our seaside treats.

This is all now being rectified by a growing number of dairy producers both north and south of the Downs. Farmers processing their own milk are matching the growing appetite for skimmed and semi-skimmed to the production of cream, much sought after in farm and community shops by local food enthusiasts. Of course it is the fat content of cream that creates the flavour, along with the source of the milk and the grazing pasture or feed. I really notice that our Sussex cream has a flavour which far exceeds that of the mass-produced alternatives.

It is, however, the increasing number of artisan ice cream makers that has really caught my eye. Look for the extra West Sussex gastro-credentials that satisfy the growing interest in local food. Caroline's Dairy is my local ice cream and their sea-buckthorne is a huge favourite of mine. From raspberry to honey, there are West Sussex flavours to challenge vanilla all the way to the bottom of the pot or cornet.

The interest in home ice cream making with the advent of domestic freeze-churn machines is massive. What makes a great homemade frozen delight is the ingredients that go into it, so local milk and cream are top of my list. Add fresh local fruit and you have something really intense in flavour and with a fabulous texture if eaten freshly churned from an ice cream machine. Make it yourself or buy it in, deliciously innovative local ice cream really can be on your year-round West Sussex menu now.

Autumn Eton Mess

I have a friend who thinks the only pudding I ever make, with seasonal fruit variations, is Eton mess. Try this autumn version and you'll understand why it is such a regular at home, topped with lovely local cream. I have never written this recipe down with quantities, but I have made it countless times. It works with however much you have of the main ingredients.

Cooking apples
Pumpkin
Raisins
Sugar
Ground nutmeg or mace
1–2 limes
Rum
Ginger cake
Custard
Meringue
West Sussex cream

1. Peel and slice the apples and pumpkin, and cook until soft with sugar and grated nutmeg, or ground mace to taste, and a very little water. Add the finely grated zest and the juice of a lime to the apple, then allow to cool. Soak some raisins in a little rum. Mix into the cooled fruit.

2. Softly whip the cream until thick but still floppy.

3. Now all you need to do is to layer up your pud in splodges. This should not be neat and tidy – just big spoonfuls of

yummy ingredients. Break up the ginger cake into the bottom of a bowl, crumble in some meringue and then splodge away. Eat within about 4 hours: it will start to become more liquid after that – still delicious but just a bit too 'messy'?

Butterscotch Sauce for Sussex Ice Cream

I think this sauce, made with local milk and butter, is perfect for any local ice cream. You do need a cooks thermometer for this – one that hasn't been in the dishwasher so that you can still see the markings on it.

50g butter
50g Demerara sugar
2 tbsp golden syrup
125ml whole milk

1. Heat the butter, sugar and syrup together slowly in a small saucepan until everything has melted and blended together.
2. Boil rapidly until the mixture reaches 115°C, or soft-ball stage (which should be marked on your thermometer).
3. Cool slightly, then gradually beat in the milk. This is delicious warm or completely cold. Stir again before serving.

Eggs

I am part of a chicken co-op: we don't actually have the birds at home but at our Community Garden in the village, where we take turns looking after them and having the eggs as a reward. It's a great scheme. A freshly laid poached egg for breakfast, with the white perfectly enrobing the yolk, is what keeping chickens is all about for me. That and the utterly amazing colour of the yolks, which comes from a variety of scraps as well as quality layers mash, and the freedom to scratch about for bugs. Happy chickens!

Whilst funky birds with feathered feet make everyone coo, in reality it is the more commercial modern hybrids that lay consistently and longest. Many of these are bred from the Sussex, a strain known to have been in the UK at the time of the Roman Conquest in AD43. We are, after all, just down the A29 from Dorking, a poultry Mecca recognised throughout the world and by an extra-

146

ordinary statue in the town. Have a little cluck about that when heading our way. The Light Sussex is now a universal favourite, but there are other Sussex strains such as the White, Speckled and Buff.

Whatever birds they keep there are plenty of egg producers in West Sussex, some large and some small. I say that not only because of the size of the operations but also because quails are laying in the county too. These tiny eggs are a cocktail and canapé favourite, and are also fabulous boiled and added to pie fillings. Local shops and pubs as well as farmers' markets sell local eggs, so you don't have to sacrifice your garden to feathered friends, unless you really want to.

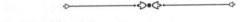

Hot and Spicy Huevos

Serves 2

This isn't really any set recipe for this because it's one of those whatever's-in-the-fridge dishes, which you can make from anything. As long as you have mashed potatoes and eggs (huevos), that is. It's based on a Tex-Mex dish called huevos rancheros, a spicy mix of refried beans, chillies and eggs with tomatoes. I always cook far too much mash whenever I make it so that we will have the potato base ready and waiting. Add other fresh veg with the pepper, and leftover veg can be added, too, with the mash.

1 red pepper
3 rashers smoked back bacon
2 tbsp olive oil
Cold mashed potato – as much as you have
Chopped chillies and olives, optional
4 large eggs

1. Prepare the pepper and slice it, and cut the bacon into strips.

2. Heat a frying pan, add the oil with the pepper and bacon, and fry until starting to brown. Add the potato with some seasoning, and fry for 5–6 minutes, turning the mixture over in the pan once or twice.

3. Pull the pan to one side and make 4 holes in the potato with the back of a large spoon. Break an egg into each and cook over a low heat for 2–3 minutes until the egg whites are setting at the bottom of the pan. Preheat the grill.

4. Place the pan under the grill for 4–5 minutes, until the eggs are set as you like them. Serve immediately – with a salad garnish if you wish or a spicy pickle, but it's fine just as it is.

Egg Mousse with Selsey Crab

Serves 6

A touch of the retro, this light and fluffy egg mayonnaise is very 1970s and very delicious. I developed the original recipe for a bridge lunch when I had a catering business and it has been a favourite ever since. Use two crabs for a more distinctive crab flavour.

(Please note: this recipe contains raw egg.)

6 large eggs
150ml mayonnaise
200g tub half fat crème fraîche
English mustard (optional)
4 sheets leaf gelatine (10g)
1 or 2 dressed Selsey crabs
2 egg whites

1. Bring the eggs to the boil in a pan of cold water, then simmer for 6 minutes. Drain the eggs and run them under cold water immediately, cracking their shells.

2. Shell the eggs and chop them finely. Mix the mayo and crème fraîche together in a bowl and season, adding a little English mustard paste if you wish. Add the chopped egg.

3. Soak the gelatine briefly in cold water as directed, then squeeze dry and dissolve in a small bowl with 3 tbsp hot water, or as directed. Stir to ensure that it has dissolved completely. Add a little of the egg mix to the dissolved gelatine, mix, then fold the gelatine into the egg mayo in the bowl. Refrigerate for 10-15 minutes, then stir in the crab meat and chill again for about 15 minutes, or until starting to show real signs of setting.

4. Whisk the egg whites until stiff then fold them into the partially set mousse. Spoon into a ring mould, or ramekins, and chill until set.

5. Serve with a salad, or with hot toast and chilli jelly.

Milk

You don't have to travel far in this beautiful county before you see a bucolic field of black-and-white dairy cows. The question is: what happens to their milk? Well, in most cases the farmers are in schemes which see the milk collected daily and taken to a major processing plant outside the county. A few farmers, however, and especially those who have chosen to keep a herd of a less-commercial breed, such as Ayrshires or Dairy Shorthorns, have opted to sell their milk to local customers.

Today it is mainly the great estates that still uphold the tradition of independent dairies. Goodwood Home Farm is the largest organic lowland farm in the UK and had the first dairy herd to be totally organically fed in the country too. The herd is Dairy Shorthorns and these beautiful cows are milked on the farm before the liquid is processed virtually next door to the parlour. The non-homogenised milk is packaged and then sold through many local outlets. Raw Goodwood milk is available on site to order and attracts an enthusiastic following. Just up the road at Midhurst the Cowdray Estate also sells its own milk and cream. More widely available is milk from Southview Farm at Bury. Southview processes its own milk on the farm, which it pasteurises and then sells, both on site and in countless village stores, restaurants and shops around the county, along with its cream. It also sells raw milk on the farm.

Any whole, or blue-top, milk, has a much better flavour and mouthfeel than semi-skimmed, because it has just over 1 per cent more cream in it, but skip homogenisation (which processes the fat particles evenly throughout the milk) and the milk truly tastes so much better as the fat is in larger particles and is tastier. Creaming off some of the fat from whole milk to make semi-skimmed and skimmed enables any dairy to also produce cream. If that cream is unhomogenised it seems to me that the larger fat particles in it trap air more readily and therefore help with hand whisking, making it quicker and easier to create a good volume of whipped cream.

Bread Pudding

Cuts into 16 pieces

I always think of hiking with the Girl Guides in the New Forest when I make this recipe. That was a long time ago, but it is still a favourite!

400g bread, crumb and crust
500ml milk
2 large eggs
250g mixed cake fruit
175g Demerara sugar
125g shredded suet
2 tsp mixed spice
Demerara sugar to finish

1. Break the bread into bite-sized pieces into a bowl, then add the milk. Cover and leave for 30 minutes or longer. Beat the mixture well to remove any lumps – I do this with a mixer but determination and a wooden spoon will do the trick. Preheat the oven to gas mark 4/180°C. Butter and/or line with baking parchment a 20cm square tin.

2. Beat the eggs and add them to the bread with all the remaining ingredients. Mix well. Add a little more milk if necessary to give a dropping consistency – the mixture should flick easily off the mixing spoon.

3. Scoop the mix into the tin and bake in the oven for 1½-1¾ hours, until a skewer poked into the middle of the mix comes out clean. Scatter with a little extra sugar and serve warm with custard, or cold as cake.

Sussex Breakfast Smoothie

Serves 3–4

A meal in itself because of the added yogurt and oats, both of which add body to this more-milk-than-fruit smoothie. Use fresh fruits of your choice, the selected seasonal combinations or about 125g frozen local summer fruits. Serve it immediately to keep the colour.

1 small banana
1 ripe peach, 3 plums, 2 apricots or 6 strawberries
75g fresh blueberries, raspberries or blackberries
1 tbsp pinhead oatmeal or 2 tbsp porridge oats
150g natural yogurt
250ml local milk

1. Peel the banana and break it into junks in a blender. Halve and remove any stones from the larger fruits and roughly chop their flesh.
2. Add all the ingredients to the banana and blend until smooth. Sweeten with a little honey if necessary, whizz again then serve.

Fish

Crab, Lobster and Other Shellfish

Walk round Pagham Harbour to Sidlesham Quay and you might well choose to reward your energetic efforts with refreshment at the Crab & Lobster, a hostelry named to sum up the history and famed produce of nearby Selsey. The shellfish capital of West Sussex, Selsey is famed not only for its lifeboats but also its brown crabs and lobsters. Pots are stacked on East Beach if they are not at work in the sea under a marker buoy, and Selsey prawns, our south coast answer to Morecambe Bay shrimps, are enjoying a tentative revival.

The poem 'The Seven Good Things of Sussex' lists Chichester as the place for lobster, but these days it is Selsey that supplies most of the mega-clawed shellfish to the county's pubs and restaurants. Blue shelled until cooked, these sought-after nippers are mainly caught from April to October, although the season really lasts all year for both crab and lobster. The summer tourists in West Sussex drive most of the trade and we are truly lucky to have such a good local supply. Lobster is so often a disappointment in both texture and flavour if it is cooked or frozen (Selsey lobsters, as far as I know, are never frozen commercially) long before it is eaten.

Crabs are actually at their best at the end of the year, and it is only the very roughest and coldest of weathers that will cause them to hide away on the seabed in the new year. Again, it is our county's tourists who drive much of the summer trade in crabs. I notice on rare trips to the fishmongers on a Saturday that you have to be there quite early, at any time of year, to get a dressed crab or two. Hand-picked crabs are what you are after, not the shells filled with mushy meat blown through with water. The dark meat will look more textured and appealing, and the shells usually look fuller from the bulkier pieces of crab. At certain times of the year the brown meat is wetter, even in hand-picked crabs, and you may need to mix it with breadcrumbs or toasted oatmeal to make a manageable sandwich filling. Most of the local boats fishing for crabs and lobsters are day boats and so the shellfish comes back to land quickly without the need for storage at sea, delivering top-quality freshness, which I believe to be essential for the texture of these wonderful shellfish.

Selsey prawns are tiny, really no more than shrimps, and so their preparation is time consuming. However, in a butter sauce atop a fine fillet of white fish they cannot be beaten, adding huge flavour from their tiny brown shapes. I cannot leave the fishmonger without some whenever I see them.

Crab and Vanilla Soup

Serves 4

Crab is rich and sweet in flavour, all of which is heightened by the addition of a vanilla pod when making this luxurious soup.

   2 dressed crabs, about 225–250g each
   1 vanilla pod
   1 potato, about 200g
   4 spring onions
   25g butter
   Good pinch of saffron strands
   500ml milk
   Smoked paprika or pimentón to garnish

1. Scrape the crab meat from the shells, and place the shells in a saucepan. Split the vanilla pod with a sharp knife, scrape out all the tiny black vanilla seeds and reserve them, then add the pod to the crab shells with 500ml cold water. Bring to the boil and simmer, uncovered, for 5 minutes. Drain the liquor and discard the shells. (Rinse the pods thoroughly, dry and keep in your caster sugar for cake making.)

2. Pick through the crab meat and reserve about 2 tbsp of chunky pieces for garnish. Peel and finely dice the potato. Trim and finely slice the spring onions.

3. Melt the butter in a large pan, add the spring onions and cook slowly for 5 minutes until softened but not browned. Add all but the reserved crab meat to the pan with the vanilla seeds, potato, saffron and milk. Bring to the boil then simmer, uncovered, for 15 minutes, until the potato is cooked.

4. Cool the soup slightly, then blend it until smooth. Season, if necessary, with salt and pepper, then add the reserved crab meat and reheat gently until piping hot. Serve garnished with a little smoked paprika.

Devilled Crab Cocktail

Serves 4 as a starter, 2 as a main course

This is a favourite recipe to demonstrate as it turns out well and causes a little gasp of pleasure at its neat layers of colourful ingredients – and it tastes as good as it looks.

  2 dressed Selsey crabs
  Small handful parsley
  1 lemon
  2 tomatoes, or 4–6 Baby Plum tomatoes
  1 ripe avocado
  2 tbsp mango chutney
  Good pinch cayenne pepper

Worcestershire sauce
Dry white breadcrumbs (optional)
Fresh bread or toast to serve

1. Scoop the white and brown crab meat into separate bowls. Finely chop the parsley and mix with the white meat, finely grating the zest from the lemon into the bowl and seasoning to taste.

2. Chop the tomatoes, seeding them if large. Chop the avocado flesh and toss it in the juice from the lemon.

3. Mix the brown meat with the chutney, cayenne pepper, seasonings and Worcestershire sauce to taste. Add breadcrumbs if the mixture is too moist – I use dried breadcrumbs, which I always have to hand.

4. Serve layered on shredded lettuce in wine glasses. Or press into well-oiled rings to shape, or into individual pudding moulds in layers, and invert immediately onto plates to serve with bread and butter or toast.

Mullet

Grey mullet is a meaty fish and is common around our shores and estuaries. The fast-flowing River Arun was once revered for the fish and the Arundel Mullet (not a gentleman's hairdressing misadventure) was renowned and was indeed one of 'The Seven Good Things of Sussex'.

Grey mullet are mature at 3–4 years and 30–35cm in length, which gives good-sized fillets of 2–3 servings each. Some fisheries forbid their capture at less than 20cm. In recent years there have been a number of Golden or Gold-spot Grey mullet in the estuaries of the county. With a distinctive golden mark behind the gills, these fish have a finer texture than common Grey mullets and I find them a delicious alternative to bass. Their flavour is clean and my recommendation is that, if you see one in your fishmongers, buy it and try it instead of bass in the Sea Bass Caesar (see page 79).

Years ago I remember watching Rick Stein cook a white fish in a red wine sauce on TV and thinking 'that's different'. Rick was actually developing a traditional recipe for a good sauce to match a stronger fish, and a red wine sauce is the basis of the traditional Arundel way to cook mullet. Poaching the fish in lightly salted water, or even with a small splash of vinegar, will help to rid it of any muddy flavour, a great tip for mullet and also for lake-caught trout. If you are lucky enough to find a Gold-spot Grey mullet, such precautions and preparations should not be necessary.

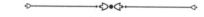

Arundel Mullet

Serves 4

With a nod to Rick Stein, here is a classic red wine sauce with mullet, the way in which the fish was traditionally served in Arundel when it was one of 'The Seven Good Things of Sussex'. Test the fish to see if it is cooked by scraping away the skin from the thickest part of the flesh on the back – if it comes away easily the mullet is done.

1 Grey mullet, about 25–30cm in length
1 onion
1 tbsp olive oil
1 lemon
1 bay leaf

200ml red wine
1 tbsp capers
Parsley and chervil or tarragon

1. Prepare the mullet so that it will fit into a large frying pan to poach – remove the head and tail if necessary. Half-fill the pan with water and add 1 tsp salt. Bring to a slow simmer then add the fish and cook slowly over a low heat for 8–12 minutes on each side according to size, turning once. Keep the mullet warm between two plates or in a warm oven. Reserve 200ml of the cooking liquor in a jug.

2. Prepare the other ingredients while the fish is poaching. Finely chop the onion, finely grate the zest from the lemon and squeeze the juice from half the fruit.

3. Reheat the pan, add the oil and the onion, and cook, with the lemon zest and bay leaf, for 5–6 minutes over a low heat until the onion is soft. Add the red wine and the reserved cooking liquor, and boil until reduced by ⅓ to ½. Add the lemon juice and capers, then season with a little salt and pepper.

4. Finely chop the parsley and chervil or tarragon, add to the sauce, stir and then season again. Add a pinch of sugar if necessary too. Lift the flesh from the bones of the mullet and reheat it, momentarily under the grill or in a hot oven, if necessary, and serve with the sauce spooned over the fish.

Roast Mullet with Orange-Buttered Greens

Serves 4

You could make this delicious dish with any white fish but the orange and the greens both have robust flavours and are well suited to mullet.

2 oranges
Small bunch of fresh dill, chervil or parsley
800g prepared spring greens
3 tbsp extra virgin olive oil
50g butter
4 pieces of Grey mullet fillet, about 150g each
200ml orange juice

1. Preheat the oven to gas mark 7/220°C and butter a shallow roasting tin.

2. Grate the zest from the oranges and set to one side, then peel the fruits and roughly chop the flesh. Finely chop the dill and finely shred the greens.

3. Bring a large pan of water to the boil, add the greens and cook for 3 minutes, then drain thoroughly in a colander. Chop the greens in the colander with a large metal spoon, which will help to expel all the water.

4. Heat the olive oil and a knob of the butter in a frying pan, then add the mullet and brown it on your chosen presentation side. Transfer the fish to the prepared tin, season and roast in the hot oven for about 6 minutes or until cooked. Reserve the buttery juices in the frying pan.

5. Add half the remaining butter to the fish juices in the frying pan, add the greens and stir-fry until soft and glossy. Remove and keep warm on a plate.

6. Add the remaining butter with the orange zest, juice and chopped orange to the frying pan, bring to the boil and then simmer until slightly reduced. Add the chopped dill and season to taste.

7. Serve the mullet on a bed of the buttered greens, with the orange sauce poured over and around the greens.

Trout and
Sussex Smokers

Think West Sussex and fish and you inevitably think of the coast and our wealth of sea species. The South Downs, however, are the source of clear-running chalk springs, which give the opportunity to create trout ponds and fisheries. With the backdrop of our beautiful rolling hills and amongst our verdant green and glorious pastures, trout fishing offers wonderfully edible recreation for the angler wishing to pit their wits against these wily fish, trying to outsmart them with their choice of fly and skill of casting.

A fine-tasting trout needs flowing water to keep the flesh clean in flavour – it also helps to spot the fly in the water and the fish being teased on to the hook. Trout, like salmon, are oily fish and therefore rich in omega-3, a nutrient which is good for our hearts and brains. Trout will take strong flavours in cooking – it is wonderful with Asian ingredients such as chillies, coriander, miso or seaweeds, ginger and soy.

Every angler will have the story of 'the one that got away and it was *this big*!'. My inclination, should I ever manage to land a trout of that size, would be to have it smoked and my first stop would be Springs at Edburton, near Henfield. This family-run smokery, established in the 1960s, is famous throughout the UK for its smoked salmon, but its shop is a Mecca for fish and local food enthusiasts alike. Springs' cures (the salting and/or spicing of the fish) and degrees of smoke are not overwhelming. The use of oak lets the natural characteristics of the fish dominate, the smoke adding flavour but not overpowering, whilst preserving at the same time. My big trout, when I catch it, will be going to Springs!

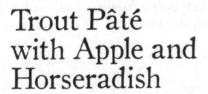

Trout Pâté with Apple and Horseradish

Serves 4–6

This pâté can actually be made with any fish, but the colour and flavour when a mix of freshly cooked and smoked trout is used is delicious. I love it in the autumn when Egremont Russet apples are in season, but it is, of course, good at any time of year.

Small bunch parsley
1 tbsp capers
1 lemon
1 large Egremont Russet apple, or a Cox or
red-skinned apple
250g crème fraîche
1–2 tbsp horseradish
350g trout, a mix of cooked and smoked is perfect

1. Wash and shake the parsley dry. Roughly chop it, then add the capers and chop again.

2. Grate the zest from ½ the lemon into a bowl, then add the juice from ½ the fruit too. Coarsely grate the apple, skin on, and toss the shreds in the lemon juice.

3. Add the crème fraîche to the bowl with the horseradish, parsley and capers, and beat until combined. Flake the trout into the mix, chopping any cold smoked trout, and stir well. Season to taste and serve on oatcakes, hot toast or on a nest of salad leaves.

Crunchy Trout Salad

Serves 6

It is the vegetables and not the fish that have the crunch! Delicious at any time of year but especially good in the winter months when a salad is a welcome change from

*swedes and cabbage, this is like a coleslaw but much
prettier to look at. Salad success comes through having
everything chopped to roughly the same size.*

125g puy lentils
50g dried cranberries
2 sticks celery
4 salad onions
½ red cabbage
Oil, e.g. olive or rapeseed
Parsley
Sugar or raisins to sweeten
Freshly cooked or smoked trout – as much as you like!

1. Wash the lentils thoroughly in a sieve, then bring them
   to the boil in a pan of water. Cover and simmer for
   15–20 minutes until just tender, or as directed on the
   packet. Drain and rinse thoroughly in cold water, and
   allow to cool.

2. Soak the cranberries in cold water until required.

3. Prepare the vegetables. Very finely slice the celery,
   chopping each stick into 4 lengthways before slicing.
   Finely slice the salad onions and place both in a bowl
   with the lentils. Cut away and discard the thick white
   of the cabbage stalk, then chop the cabbage very finely.
   This would be simplest in a food processor. Drain the
   cranberries and squeeze them dry, then chop them
   roughly. Add to the lentils with the red cabbage.

4. Season the salad well. Finely chop the parsley and add it just before serving, with sufficient oil to moisten the vegetables. Add a little sugar too, if you wish, or some raisins for their natural sweetness. Flake the cooked trout, or shred roughly if using smoked, and mix into the salad just before serving.

Unusual Fish

Hugh Fearnley-Whittingstall and his team have been hugely successful in raising our awareness of fish species other than cod and haddock. For the small fishing companies this is most welcome: if there is a market for everything in the net it makes for a much more sustainable business, and there is a real and growing appetite for local fish from day boats working along our coast.

In plentiful supply are West Sussex cuttlefish and squid. Before preparation they look very different, with cuttlefish being quite beautifully coloured. They are unique as the cuttle is an internal bone, the flat oval pecking delight given to pet caged birds, or found littered over our shingle beaches after winter storms. The flesh that we eat is cut into squid-like rings and is cooked in a similar way, if for a little longer. West Sussex squid are not the biggest in the world but they are delicious. I like to buy them at about 300–400g, which gives good-sized pieces of tender flesh. Many oriental cuisines open out squid tubes – the pockets of flesh left after cleaning and skinning – and cut them into large pieces for stir-frying. I always cook them in rings – quickly over a high heat, or long and slow in a rich sauce until meltingly tender. I try to prepare a squid in cookery demonstrations as often as possible as it is easy to do and interesting to watch.

Ink is used by octopi, squid and cuttlefish for defence, and they eject it to cloud the water when up against predators. Squid ink is actually blue-black, like standard Quink, and it is the black ink of octopi that is truly best for making black pasta.

Eels, once plentiful in West Sussex, were usually boiled and then jellied in their own stock. The Pulborough eel pudding has a suet crust, with a filling of chopped filleted eels mixed with hard-boiled eggs and pickled pork or bacon, plus a liquor made from the eel trimmings, some onion and chopped parsley. I think that sounds great for a winter's day, but over-fishing of these mysterious creatures has meant a voluntary ban on their capture until their numbers are increased, which is slowly starting to happen.

Squid Goulash

Serves 2

Forget tough, chewy squid rings in batter in a basket. Cooked like this in a rich tomato sauce and spiced with paprika, squid is a gourmet's delight.

350g prepared squid
1 onion
1 carrot
1 stick celery
1 clove garlic
2 red chillies
2 tbsp fruity olive oil
2 tsp sweet or Hungarian paprika
½ tsp picante or smoked paprika (optional)
2 bay leaves
400ml passata/sieved tomatoes or 400g can
chopped tomatoes

1. Leave the squid tentacles whole and cut the tubes or bodies into rings no more than 1cm thick. Finely dice the onion, carrot and celery, and finely chop the garlic and chillies.

2. Heat a saucepan, add the oil then the squid and cook for 2–3 minutes until the flesh becomes opaque. Add the onion, carrot and celery with the paprika and bay leaves, and cook for a further 2 minutes over a medium

173

heat. Add the garlic and chillies with the tomatoes and bring to the boil, then cover and simmer slowly for 45 minutes to 1 hour. Add a little water if the sauce becomes too thick.

3. Remove the bay leaves and season to taste. Serve with rice or pasta, or as it is with bread.

Salt and Chilli Squid

Serves 2–3

This is a warm salad – unusually featuring hot radishes – and it is all about heat and spice.

2 chillies, one red and one green
2 cloves garlic
12 radishes
1 carrot
Small bunch coriander
1 lime
350g squid rings
1 tbsp sunflower seeds
2 tbsp oil for frying – groundnut and rapeseed are good
Sea salt flakes

1. Seed then finely chop the chillies with the garlic. Slice the radishes and cut the carrot into very fine batons

about 5cm long. Roughly chop the coriander and grate the lime zest onto it. Squeeze the juice from the lime.

2. Heat a large frying pan or wok and add the oil. Add the squid rings and stir-fry quickly for 3 minutes or so, until starting to colour. Add the radishes and carrot, stir, then add the chilli and garlic, and cook for a further minute. Toss in the sunflower seeds and the lime juice, bubble then pile on to hot plates with the juices spooned over.

3. Mix a good pinch of sea salt flakes with the coriander and lime zest, and scatter over the squid as you serve.

White Fish

A thick loin of Channel cod: is that a memory of yesteryear, a reckless indulgence or a firm favourite on our menus for many years to come? The good news is that the conservation no-catch areas for cod over the latter years of the noughties have been an unmitigated success and cod stocks around our coasts are at very healthy levels again. West Sussex cod has always been popular – as consumers we just cannot get enough of the pearlescent white flakes of juicy, succulent fish. However, while cod was off the menu we have been introduced to or reacquainted with many other white fish and I think this has broadened our piscatorial creativity considerably.

Pollack and whiting are members of the cod family, and pollock, when it is truly fresh, delivers on flesh colour and flavour for cod lovers. Whiting is sweet and delicious grilled with a chilli butter garnish melting into the fillets.

Ask any beach fisherman what they are hoping to catch and you'll probably be talking to someone in pursuit of a bass. Sea bass have become very popular in the past decade or so, yielding good meaty flesh that takes the flavour of herbs and capers well. Sea bream, also plentiful off our coast, are best filleted and pin-boned for you. They are often on local restaurant menus.

The flatfish off our coast, especially in the west of the county, are top quality. Plaice, with its smart orange spots, Dover and lemon soles, brill and turbot all favour the shallower waters over sandbanks. Grilled or pan fried, there is little that delights me more than a fillet of brill. Turned in oatmeal and fried in butter. Gorgeous. Skate, or ray, is also a big favourite in our house. There has been a conservation issue with these fish too, again addressed. I usually choose thick wings and fillet them for the recipe which follows, or turn the wings in seasoned flour and cook them in olive oil before adding capers, parsley, black pepper and butter.

A trip to one of our excellent local fishmongers may bring yet more local surprises. Red gurnard, once only used as lobster bait, is now widely regarded as a gourmet's choice and is fabulous in fish stews. A good fishmonger will fillet it for you in no time: it is very difficult to do yourself. My biggest surprise to date came in the form of some topknots – flatfish about the size of a dab but with the flesh of a brill. They were completely delicious and are caught occasionally by our local day boats. A great pleasure for me is to ask my fishmonger to prepare a fish box from the local catch. I never mind what is in it and love the challenge of deciding how to cook each delicious species from our West Sussex waters.

Baked Cod with Apple and Cheese

Serves 4

This recipe is always popular at demonstrations and is great for entertaining as it can be prepared in advance and just baked when needed. Cook the shallots and set to one side, ready to reheat with the fruit. Turn the apples in a little lemon juice if not making the salad immediately.

4 pieces of cod fillet, about 200g each
2 Cox or other crisp red-skinned apples
3 tbsp hazelnuts or cobnuts in season
1 shallot
Parsley
50g Sussex Cheddar-style cheese
3 tbsp dry white breadcrumbs
2 tbsp olive oil

1. Preheat the oven to gas mark 6/200°C. Season the cod lightly. Cut the apples into 6mm dice, roughly chop the hazelnuts and finely chop the shallot and the parsley. Grate the cheese and mix it with the breadcrumbs and a little seasoning.

2. Heat a large non-stick frying pan, add the oil, then add the fish, flesh down, and cook for 2–3 minutes until browned. Turn, and place in an ovenproof dish. Scatter the cheese mix over the top and bake for 10 minutes.

3. Add the shallot to the juices in the pan and cook slowly for 2–3 minutes. Add the apple and continue cooking until just starting to soften, then add the nuts. Cook for 1 minute more, then season and add most of the parsley.
4. Serve the cod with the warm apple salad on the side, scattered with the remaining parsley.

Crispy Fried Skate with Shredded Ginger Salad

Serves 4

This is a recipe for the deep-fryer, although you could also fry the fish in a wok in less oil. Do try it – it is exotic yet simple despite needing a lot of ingredients.

1 small celeriac
2 carrots
2 sticks celery
½ cucumber
5cm fresh root ginger
1 clove garlic
3 tbsp sunflower oil
2 tbsp toasted sesame oil
2 tbsp soy sauce
1 tsp poppy seeds

800g–1kg ray or skate wing
1 large egg white
3 tbsp double cream
100g flour
½ tsp salt
½ tsp mild chilli powder
1 tsp ground ginger
Oil for deep-frying

1. Prepare the vegetables. Grate the carrot and celeriac coarsely by hand, or on a medium plate on a food processor. Seed the cucumber, then slice it and the celery finely.

2. Coarsely grate the ginger with the skin, then gather it up in your hand and squeeze the juice into a large bowl. Crush the garlic into the bowl, then add the oils, soy sauce and poppy seeds, and whisk into a dressing. Add the vegetables and toss together.

3. Heat the oil in a deep-fat fryer to 180°C. Cut the fish from the bones and then into 2½cm pieces. Whisk the egg white and cream together in a bowl until combined, then rub the mixture into the fish. Mix the flour and seasonings together on a plate.

4. Coat the fish in the flour, then gently lower the pieces into the hot oil and fry for 3–4 minutes, until golden brown. Do this in two batches so that the pieces of fish do not stick together and the oil does not loose temperature. Drain the fish well on crumpled kitchen paper, then serve on a bed of the salad with coarse sea salt sprinkled over.

Meat
& Game

Bacon

The meat most likely to make a carnivore of a vegetarian!
A good bacon, with a mix of savoury and fatty tastes, is
the closest food to the holy grail of flavour, umami. The
never-ending search for leaner meat has stolen a lot from
the delight of a bacon rasher. Lean is all very well, but
for the true flavour of bacon some fat is required – and I
like mine as crispy as possible. This is most often achieved
in bacon cured from traditional breeds of pigs, when the
back or loin, collar or belly are slowly processed with a
traditional dry curing mix.

There are two ways of making bacon: with a wet cure
or a dry cure. The latter is the slow, traditional method;
the former the 'do it quick and do it cheap' panacea for
our cut-price, quick-serve lifestyle. A wet cure involves
steeping pieces of pork in a vat of brine – and the same
solution is often injected into the meat too – to hasten
the curing or preserving process. A dry cure involves

rubbing the meat with salt and leaving it to penetrate, drawing out the juices and thus preserving the meat. Every single nook and cranny of the pork must be rubbed with the salt cure to ensure no fresh meat is left untreated, as it would harbour bacteria and spoil the bacon.

I've had several attempts now at curing my own bacon and it is not as easy as it sounds. My advice therefore is to find a bacon expert and support them. If they keep pigs and produce all sorts of pork you might occasionally be able to buy a bacon hock from them as well as rashers: they make the most delicious change from ham and are particularly wonderful with beans – with broad beans in salad, with butter beans in casseroles or even with baked beans as a pub lunch. You might have to cut off your own rind if you buy bacon rashers from a small producer, but the birds will love you for them!

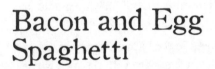

Bacon and Egg Spaghetti

Serves 2

Yes, a carbonara, but there is always fierce debate about cream or no cream, and whether to cook the eggs at all before adding them to the pasta. This is my West Sussex take on the Italian classic.

4 rashers smoked back bacon
1 clove garlic
4 large eggs
2–3 tbsp milk or double cream
1–2 tbsp freshly grated Parmesan
200–250g spaghetti
1 tbsp olive oil plus a knob of butter
Chopped parsley to garnish

1. Cut the bacon into strips and crush the garlic. Beat the eggs with the milk or cream and some seasoning, then add the Parmesan.

2. Bring a large pan of salted water to the boil, add the spaghetti and boil for 10 minutes, or as directed on the packet.

3. Heat the oil and butter together in a frying pan, add the bacon and garlic, and cook over a moderate heat until the bacon is starting to brown. Reduce the heat, pour in the eggs and cook gently until they are just beginning to set, stirring frequently. Drain the spaghetti in a colander.

4. Toss the hot spaghetti in the bacon and egg in the pan, then pile onto plates and garnish with chopped parsley.

Hock and Broad Bean Salad with Pesto

This is a wonderful way of using up the leftover meat from a cured ham or bacon hock. The real point of this recipe is the pesto. This is classic pesto Genovese, the delicious sauce of Genoa.

For the pesto:

A large handful of basil leaves – a few stalks
are OK, but not too many
40–50g freshly grated Parmesan
40–50g pine nuts
2–3 cloves garlic
100ml extra virgin olive oil (approx.)

Cooked broad beans
Chunks of bacon from a hock (or ham)
Lettuce leaves

1. The quantities for any part of this recipe are not truly important – I am a firm believer that if you make pesto with the right ingredients it will always be delicious, even if the quantities vary slightly. Taste and texture are subjective – and are also sometimes dictated by what you have to hand!

2. Whizz the pesto ingredients up in a blender to a paste, adding a little salt and extra oil if required. The pesto remaining after the salad can be poured into a warm clean jar, sealed and kept in the fridge for 2–3 weeks.

3. Prepare the lettuce and arrange on a platter with the ham and beans. I wouldn't season the ingredients as there is so much flavour buzz in the pesto. Drizzle the pesto over the salad and serve with hunks of bread. Rustic eating at its best.

Beef

Beef: quintessentially British and our local breed is amongst the finest for eating quality.

The Sussex is amongst the oldest English cattle, known to be big and hard workers, and often draft beasts for ploughing. Their size was often great, and a big selling point for farmers needing a strong animal to work hard. I feel a great affinity with these magnificent creatures myself, never having been a skinny cook!

My friend Jack raises Sussex cattle on his farm at Stopham, but he is just one of 28 farmers registered with the Sussex Cattle Society as having pure Sussex animals. This is fantastic news for local beef lovers as the meat is truly delicious. The breed is, however, much less common than both Aberdeen Angus and Hereford, and it deserves far greater recognition than it has.

In the west of the county there is a small group of farmers raising salt marsh-grazed cattle under the brand of Three Harbours Beef. Cattle are grazed in Pagham,

Chichester and Langstone harbours, and along the coastal strip around and about the harbour inlets. Much of the land grazed is within the Chichester Harbour Conservancy, an area of Outstanding Natural Beauty. Salt marsh grazing has long been used to create some of the tastiest mutton and lamb, and it works really well with beef too. Brisket from these cattle is a fabulous feast. As with all specialist schemes, much of the Three Harbours Beef is sold through beef boxes from their own HQ, but a growing number of restaurants, including the Cloisters Cafe at Chichester Cathedral, feature the beef on their menus, and some farm shops and butchers sell it too.

Beef and Coconut Curry

Serves 4

This recipe was inspired by a visit to Kerala in south-west India. You could use the curry paste of your choice instead of the spice combination below, but these seasonings work well together. Serve the curry with boiled rice, naan breads or chapattis and chutney, or lime pickle if you like it hot!

1 large onion
1 carrot
1 sweet potato

1 red chilli
1 clove garlic
100g creamed coconut
2 tbsp oil
1 tsp each of cumin and fennel seeds
6 each of green cardamoms, cloves and black peppercorns
500g braising steak
1 tsp ground turmeric
200ml water
400g can chopped tomatoes
1 large cinnamon stick
1 tsp salt
Freshly chopped coriander to garnish

1. Prepare the vegetables. Dice the onion and cut the carrot and sweet potato into 2–3cm pieces. Finely chop the chilli with the garlic. Roughly chop the creamed coconut.

2. Heat a large pan and add the oil. Add the whole spices and cook for a few seconds until fragrant, then add the beef and turmeric and stir-fry briefly for 1–2 minutes. Stir in the onions with the water, cover the pan and cook over a low heat for 5 minutes.

3. Add the diced vegetables with the chopped chilli, garlic and coconut, and stir until the latter has melted. Add the tomatoes with the cinnamon and salt. Bring to the boil, stir and cover, then simmer very slowly or cook in a low oven at gas mark 3/160°C for at least 2 hours, until the beef is tender. A longer cook of 3–4 hours

in the oven will be fine, but add a little more water if necessary.

4. Season to taste and garnish with coriander.

Oyster Beef with Vegetable Noodles

Serves 4

My favourite kind of winter cooking – a long slow cook with a quick flourish of a finish!

2 onions
4 tbsp groundnut or sunflower oil
4 thick pieces of braising steak, about 150g each
2 cloves garlic
1 cinnamon stick
2 pieces star anise
150ml bottle oyster sauce
3 tbsp soy sauce
2 red peppers
2 green peppers
1 bunch spring onions
375g pack medium egg noodles
2 tbsp toasted sesame oil

1. Preheat the oven to gas mark 3/160°C. Prepare the onions and cut them into quarters.

2. Heat 2 tbsp oil in a large flameproof casserole and brown the beef on both sides. Add the onions and crush the garlic into the pan, then add the cinnamon, star anise, and the oyster and soy sauces. Rinse the oyster sauce bottle out with water and add that to the pan too, to cover the beef. Bring to the boil, then cover and cook in the preheated oven for a minimum of 3–4 hours.

3. Prepare the peppers and cut them into strips. Trim the spring onions and slice them diagonally. Prepare the noodles as directed on the packet.

4. Heat a wok and then add the remaining oil to it. Add the peppers and stir-fry for 1–2 minutes, then add the onions and cook for a further 1 minute. Drain the noodles, shake dry and toss in the sesame oil, then add the noodles to the wok and toss them with the vegetables.

5. Season the beef and boil the sauce to reduce it slightly if necessary, then serve on a bed of the vegetable noodles.

Delicatessen Meats

Ham and gammon: what is the difference? Both are wet cured, but come from the front and rear legs of the pig respectively. Steeped in brine for at least 48 hours, they might then be further processed in cider, beer, treacle, honey and spices. I can find no reference to a traditional Sussex cure but I would hazard a guess that a great many hams in Sussex might have steeped in cider over the years. The art of a good ham is to ensure that it is not salty. Smoked or not, nothing will cover up excessive salt. There are masters of ham curing and cooking in our county. The cooking is critical too. Ham must be cooked through, but overcook it and it will be dry and tough to the bite. Carved from the bone a good ham takes some beating – it was always a bestseller in our deli. My favourite locally produced ham comes from Adsdean Farm near Funtington. This local meat mecca has been selling their home produced meats for decades, fresh and for the freezer.

Pâtés, terrines and parfaits are often made by keen delicatessen owners and sold by the slice to appreciative customers. You are more likely to find these in independent shops or on restaurant and pub menus. Find a pub serving a home-made pâté that you enjoy and you might be able to buy a slice to take home. Parfaits, light, creamy and mousse-like, are the most difficult to get right in my opinion. A parfait of chicken livers with some ceps layered into it is a treat indeed, and it's the type of deli delight that I want to buy and not make myself! A little, occasionally, is wonderful.

Our traditional UK sausages tend to be of the fresh variety, and not the dried or smoked kinds so popular in Europe. However, the increasing use of salamis and chorizos on TV cookery programmes, and their widespread availability in supermarkets, has made us much more curious about and adventurous with these preserved meats. I have had great success with home-made chorizos, where the pork is preserved with red wine, pimentón, garlic and pepper, and then dried.

West Sussex Paella

Serves 4

The first time that I wrote a recipe for paella was for a cookbook for the TV series Emmerdale – *Annie, one of the characters, had moved to Spain. This variation includes the hams and spicy sausages that we have in West Sussex.*

1 large onion
1 green and 1 red pepper
1–2 red chillies
1–2 cloves garlic
3–4 tomatoes
150g cooked ham
2–3 large spicy pork sausages
3 tbsp oil
1 tsp smoked paprika
250g paella or risotto rice
150ml white wine
600ml boiling stock
1 dressed Selsey crab
Parsley to garnish

1. Chop the onion and slice the peppers. Seed then finely chop the chillies with the garlic. Roughly chop the tomatoes. Roughly chop the ham. Thickly slice the sausages.

2. Heat a large frying pan, add the oil, then the sausage slices and brown them quickly on both sides. Add the

prepared vegetables with the paprika and cook over a medium heat for 2–3 minutes. Stir in the rice, coating it in the spicy oil, then add the wine and bubble for a minute or so.

3. Stir in the stock and simmer the paella, stirring frequently, until it is half absorbed in about 10 minutes, then add the ham. Continue cooking until the stock is all but gone and the rice is almost tender (add a little more liquid if necessary during cooking), then add the crab meat. Cook for a further 2–3 minutes to heat the crab right through.

4. Season to taste, then serve scattered with freshly chopped parsley.

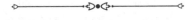

Pork Terrine with Bacon

Serves 8

Pig's liver is perfect in pâtés. A terrine is usually a coarse mix of meat and liver, baked in bacon and then pressed until cold. I usually make one of these each time we despatch our pigs – it's a great favourite at community garden suppers.

6 rashers streaky bacon
600–650g belly pork

1 onion
1–2 cloves garlic
½ a pig's liver, about 350–400g
1 tsp dried thyme or 1 tbsp fresh leaves, roughly chopped
3 tbsp brandy or damson gin

1. Preheat the oven to gas mark 4/180°C. Remove the rind from the bacon and stretch the rashers lightly with the back of a knife. Arrange them over the base and sides of a 1kg loaf tin, leaving the ends trailing over the sides of the tin.

2. Remove the rind from the belly pork and cut it into strips. Peel and roughly chop the onion and garlic. Dice half the liver very finely, then mince the remainder with the belly pork, onion and garlic. Turn into a bowl and add the thyme, the chopped liver and plenty of salt and pepper, then moisten with the brandy or gin.

3. Pile the mixture into the prepared tin, smooth the top, then fold the ends of the bacon rashers over the filling. Cover with foil and place in a deep roasting tin. Pour boiling water into the tin to come halfway up the sides of the loaf tin. Carefully set the roasting tin in the oven.

4. Bake for 1½ hours. Carefully remove from the oven and leave to cool completely, out of the water bath. Place a heavy weight on top of the foil, then refrigerate the terrine in the tin for 4 hours or overnight. Serve sliced, with pickles or chutney, a small salad and bread or toast.

Lamb and Mutton

I feel that I have noticed far more sheep on the Downs in the past few years. Certainly that would tie in with our wish to know where our food comes from and to eat local meat whenever possible. The sheep are great conservation workers, perfect for grazing on the thin but beautiful goodness of the South Downs.

The Southdown breed are small in size but have played a big part in the husbandry of the Downs. Originally they grazed the hills in the daytime and were taken down into the valleys for safety at night, where they manured the poor soils, improving the ground for crops. Their meat was valued, but so were their fleeces. The breed then lost out to larger animals, which yielded bigger carcasses, and became listed with the Rare Breeds Survival Trust. This conservation has paid off and the breed appears secure again, with 22 farmers having pure Southdown sheep in West Sussex. I find the meat sweet in flavour and succulent in the mouth. A well-reared lamb should never be excessively fatty, although a thin layer of fat is needed both to flavour the meat and to protect it from drying out during cooking.

There are three ages of sheep meat: lamb, hogget and mutton. There is confusion about definitions and so I am going to give you mine – they may cause debate with farmers around your dinner table but they work for me! Lamb is the meat from an animal under six months old. Hogget, a term not much heard and which might also be referred to as autumn lamb, is meat from an animal between six and 12 months at slaughter. Mutton can be anything older than that, although I always try to buy it between 18–24 months old. Lamb obviously will need less cooking than mutton and may be served quite pink if that is to your taste. Mutton should always be cooked through. Many people say mutton can be unpalatably strong but I have never once found that. In my experience mutton from West Sussex tastes of nothing but good pasture! Ask for it at farmers' markets, but you might have to order in advance.

Minted Lamb and Potato Moussaka

Serves 4–6

Local ingredients can be used to cook in the style of any cuisine. I am always surprised at the sunshine flavours of this selection of local ingredients. Try replacing the potato with squash in season.

1 large onion
2 cloves garlic
750g potatoes
1 handful fresh mint leaves
500g minced lamb
½ tsp dried oregano or 1 tbsp fresh leaves
150ml dry white wine
400g can chopped tomatoes
2 tbsp tomato purée
500g Greek-style yogurt
2 large eggs

1. Prepare the vegetables. Finely chop the onion and crush the garlic. Cut the peeled potatoes into 75–100g pieces. Roughly chop the mint.

2. Heat a large pan, add the lamb and cook quickly to draw the fat from the meat. Add the chopped onion with the oregano, reduce the heat and cook for 5–6 minutes, until the onion is softened. Add the garlic

199

and the wine and bubble for 3–4 minutes, then add the tomatoes and tomato purée. Stir in the mint with some salt and pepper, then simmer for 20 minutes, or until reduced to a thick sauce.

3. Preheat the oven to gas mark 6/200°C. Bring the potatoes to the boil in cold water, then cover and simmer for 15 minutes while the lamb is cooking. Drain and allow to cool slightly, then cut into thick slices.

4. Season the lamb, then spoon half into the bottom of a large baking dish and top with half the potato. Repeat the layers. Beat the yogurt with the eggs and a little salt and pepper, then top the moussaka with the mixture.

5. Set the dish on a baking tray then bake in the hot oven for 30–40 minutes, until the topping has set. Serve with fresh green vegetables, or a tomato, onion and feta cheese salad.

Late-Summer Mutton Stew

Serves 4

A perfect recipe for September, but adaptable for any season's vegetable bounty.

3 onions
2–3 leeks

1 small butternut squash
500g tomatoes
4–6 anchovy fillets
2 tbsp rapeseed or olive oil
500g shoulder of mutton, diced
Water or vegetable stock
1 sweet red pepper
250g mixed beans – runners, broad and
green beans, fresh or frozen
2–3 tbsp basil pesto

1. Slice the onions and leeks thinly, then seed, peel and finely dice the squash. Roughly chop the tomatoes and the anchovy fillets.

2. Heat a large flameproof casserole on the hob, add the oil, onions, leeks and squash, and cook, covered, over a low heat for 5 minutes, stirring from time to time. Add the mutton and cook until browned, then add the tomatoes and anchovies with sufficient water or vegetable stock to just cover the meat. Bring to a simmer, then cover and cook slowly for 3 hours for mutton – if you use lamb it will cook in about 2 hours – either on a very low simmer or in an oven preheated to gas mark 3/160°C.

3. Chop the sweet pepper into 1cm dice and add it to the pan with the beans. Continue to simmer for a further 10 minutes, or until cooked to your liking.

4. Stir the pesto into the pan just before serving, then season with extra salt and pepper if necessary. I found that the flavour of the mutton and vegetables combined with the pesto required very little extra seasoning at all.

The South Downs National Park

The South Downs National Park, the newest of Britain's treasured open spaces, stretches right across West Sussex, taking in 41 per cent of the county which, in turn, makes up 49 per cent of the Park. This newly protected area of conservation and recreation for all is massively important for our glorious countryside and surroundings, but how will it affect our food?

Farming is an essential part of life in the Park, as it not only provides food for us but also habitats for ground-nesting birds, rare butterflies and other wildlife – some of which we do eat, like pheasants and deer. The richer and more diverse the wildlife, the better the crops will be, as long as the wildlife is managed and does not get out of balance. The Park is building a distinct identity and, as this develops, it should provide a provenance marque or brand that will be applied to everything produced within its boundaries, although it is likely to cover much more than just food. Crafts, traditional charcoal, duvets made of sheep's wool and food and drink: all these artisan goods share their rootedness in the Park.

What excites me most about the potential for local food in the South Downs National Park is the huge number of opportunities that it offers to promote our local fare. Farmers' markets in Midhurst and Petworth, and fabulous food shops along the Downs all play their part as retail opportunities, but the leisure-based chances to encounter some local food and drink are manifold. You would almost have to get lost on the Downs without a map to avoid a pub, tea shop or hotel with some local food or drink on its menu!

Traditional pubs, with lots of character and a great selection of local beers, crop up with almost planned regularity along the byways criss-crossing the Park. Of course, their original purpose was to provide refreshment for travellers and, with the huge interest in walking in West Sussex, especially along the South Downs Way, Monarch's Way and Downs Link, and the Wey South path, the demand for good, local and seasonal pub food is growing, and will surely continue to grow.

The National Park is already concentrating on recreational refreshment information, and has produced at least one leaflet of walks and trails around West Sussex, with places of interest and suitable hostelries highlighted along the ways. Look out for it in featured pubs, tourist information offices and on National Park stands at shows across the county.

Partridge and Pheasant

Partridge is the first local game to come into season in the autumn. Grouse (not to be found alive in West Sussex) open the season on 12 August and partridge follow on from 1 September until shooting ends on 1 February, the same day as the end of the pheasant season. This amazes me, as I am never so aware of partridge once the pheasant season begins. There are two varieties of partridge, the Grey, which is our traditional breed, and the Red-legged, which is more colourful and bred from birds of European descent. The flavour of partridge is that of a slightly gamey chicken, not much deeper in flavour than a guineafowl. It is delicate and a treat. Partridge takes complementary flavours readily but you have to be careful not to swamp its delicate taste with other stronger ingredients. Subtlety is required, and in accompanying wines as well. True gourmets might eat partridge pink but I cannot. If I roast it, unless the birds are very young and one a serving per person, I like to take the legs and thighs off the bird and start them cooking before adding the breasts, which I keep on the bone. That way I can have everything perfectly cooked with the breasts moist but the legs cooked through. There are many who would just cook the breasts, as there is little meat on the legs. What there is, however, is great finger food – or alternatively good for stocks.

Pheasant are bigger birds and easier to cook. The flavour is more developed, the meat is darker and it is altogether more robust. Pheasant shooting begins on 1 October and good bargains may be had if you have access to a shoot at the end of the season. Remember, however, that you will be buying birds in feather and the dressing will be up to you. I love pheasant casseroles with lots of winter vegetables and spices, and it makes great curries too. The breasts can be smoked and I think this is another delicatessen meat that should be produced here in West Sussex. Smoked pheasant, watercress and walnut mayo sandwiches in winter? Yes please!

Partridge with Black Pudding, Figs and Apples

Serves 4

A fabulous way of serving game – it's great with pheasant or guineafowl breasts too. Use cobnuts in season and hazelnuts at other times.

4 or 8 partridge breasts, depending on size
1 large onion
50g soft dried figs
1 Cox eating apple
50g hazelnuts
2 cloves garlic
1 small bunch parsley
250g black pudding or haggis
1–2 tbsp olive oil
150ml damson gin or red wine, such as Rioja
25g butter
Chopped hazelnuts and raisins to garnish

1. Preheat the oven to gas mark 6/200°C. Thinly slice the onion, roughly chop the figs, apple and hazelnuts, crush the garlic and finely chop the parsley. Peel and crumble the black pudding.

2. Melt the butter in a large frying pan, add the onions and cook slowly until soft and golden. Stir in the parsley,

garlic, figs, apples and crumbled black pudding with the chopped nuts. Mix well and season lightly, then turn most of it into the base of a buttered ovenproof dish.

3. Heat the oil in the frying pan and brown the partridge breasts quickly on both sides. Lay on top of the black pudding mix, then scatter the remainder over the top. Pour the damson gin over, cover with foil and cook in the preheated oven for 20–25 minutes. Stand for 5 minutes before serving – delicious with green veg.

Braised Pheasant with Lentils, Prunes and Pickled Walnuts

Serves 4

My all-time-favourite way of cooking pheasant and I hope that you like it too. The pickled walnuts just lift the seasoning of the dish.

4 pheasant breasts
2 tbsp seasoned flour
4 rashers smoked streaky bacon
1 large onion
1 large carrot
4 stalks celery, chopped
2 tbsp olive oil

2 tsp dried rosemary
2 bay leaves
200ml dry white wine
400ml stock (approx.)
8 pitted prunes
75g green lentils
8–10 pickled walnuts

1. Remove the breasts from 2 large pheasants, or buy them ready done. Turn the pheasant in the seasoned flour (plain flour with salt and black pepper). Finely chop the bacon, onion, carrot and celery.

2. Heat a deep sauté pan, then add the oil and the pheasant breasts, and brown them quickly on both sides. Remove the pheasant with a slotted spoon, add the prepared vegetables, then cover and cook slowly for 5 minutes.

3. Add the wine to the pan and bring to the boil, scraping up any sediment from the bottom of the pan. Return the browned pheasant to the pan with the seasonings and add enough stock to cover. Stir in the prunes and lentils. Bring to the boil then simmer, half covered, for 45 minutes or until both the pheasant and the lentils are tender.

4. Slice the pickled walnuts thickly, add them to the pan and heat through for 2–3 minutes. Season to taste before serving, perhaps with a creamy mash with celeriac in it.

Pork

Whilst the majority of commercial outdoor pork in the UK is raised on much sandier soils than we have in West Sussex – pigs hate having their trotters up to their knuckles in mud – we still have our share of excellent pig rearers who are producing top-quality pork in macro and medium-sized businesses.

The most common breed of pig to see on a commercial unit will be the Large White, which has a long back and provides good-sized joints for bacon. You will often see such pigs in the fields at Funtington, and in a few other areas where a field or two with regularly spaced corrugated metal arcs will be a sure sign of porcine occupation. However, most of the smaller breeders in the county favour traditional breeds that command a premium and are ready sooner. If a breed like a Saddleback matures much beyond eight or nine months they are a challenge on conformation, or fat-to-meat ratio. There is also the issue of butchery too: if the pigs become too large many butchers simply cannot physically cope with manipulating the large carcasses. The smaller carcasses are ideal for hog roasts too, and several West Sussex pig keepers have good outdoor catering businesses around the county, up into London and beyond.

All that is practicality. The flavour of traditional breeds like Saddlebacks and Gloucester Old Spots is really what sells the meat to us. They are slightly slower growing than modern commercial breeds and, whilst having a good coating of fat to the prime roasting joints, if the point of slaughter is correct, the fat cover will be perfect for flavour and not too much for other cuts. The crackling from traditional breeds is wonderful because of the greater depth of fat over the roasting joints – is there anything better than a roast loin of pork?

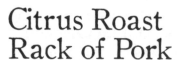

Citrus Roast Rack of Pork

Serves 4–6

Pork is of top quality in the first months of the year, when citrus fruits are at their best too. The flavour of this roast is really special.

1½kg loin or rack of pork, trimmed by the butcher

1 tbsp coarse sea salt, plus a little extra
1 tsp Chinese 5 spice powder
1 orange
2 lemons
1 tbsp fresh sage leaves (optional)
500ml well-flavoured stock

1. Preheat the oven to gas mark 7/220°C. Score the crackling on the pork finely – very few butchers or retailers do this properly. Using a sharp knife, cut down through the fat but not right through to the muscle below. Carefully loosen the fat from the muscle, peeling it backwards away from the bones – do not detach it completely. Finely grate the citrus zests and chop the sage if using. Squeeze the juice from the orange and reserve it.

2. Mix 1 tbsp salt with the 5 spice, citrus rinds and sage, then press the mixture over the pork and press the scored crackling back into place. Roast in the hot oven for 15 minutes, then reduce the temperature to gas mark 5/190°C and roast for a further 1½ hours.

3. Allow the pork to stand for 10 minutes. Make the gravy while the pork is standing by adding the stock to the meat juices in the roasting tin and simmering until well reduced. Add the orange juice and heat gently before seasoning. Remove the bones completely from the pork, then slice thinly and serve with the orange gravy, roast potatoes and vegetables.

Autumn Pork

Serves 4

I have always loved to mix meat and fruit in my recipes. It works so well in this dish, where the apple helps to make a lovely sauce for the casserole too. You could just simmer this slowly on the hob until the meat is tender in roughly the same cooking time if you prefer.

750g mixed casserole vegetables, e.g. leek, parsnip, swede, carrots
250g mixed dried fruits, e.g. apricots, apples, pears, prunes
1 large Bramley apple
2 tbsp olive oil
500g leg of pork, diced
1 tsp ground mace or 2 whole blades of mace
500ml cider or apple juice
Chives or parsley to garnish

1. Preheat the oven to gas mark 5/190°C.
2. Prepare the vegetables and chop into 1½cm slices or dice. Roughly chop the dried fruits. Peel, core and slice the Bramley.
3. Heat the oil in a flameproof casserole, add the pork and brown on all sides. Add the mace and prepared vegetables. Cook for 3–4 minutes, then add the fruits, seasonings and cider or apple juice. Bring to the boil,

cover and transfer to the hot oven for 1½ hours. You could simmer this slowly for an hour or so if you prefer.

4. Season to taste, adding a little sugar if necessary with salt and pepper. Garnish with chives or parsley and serve with creamy mustard mashed potatoes and green vegetables.

Sausages

What makes a good sausage? It is, of course, a matter of taste, but I do believe that size matters when it comes to bangers and big is beautiful when sausages are under consideration. The downside of the size debate is the length of time needed to cook the sausages through properly. I'm happy with chipolatas for breakfast but it has to be a big banger at other times for me. The best sausages are always made with good meat. Shoulders will produce a great balance of muscle with just a little fat for the almost perfect sausage, but other forequarter meat can go into the mix as well.

Of course, pork is not the only meat for the banger and I love to see seasonal variations with pheasant and lamb included, as well as venison, which makes a fabulous sausage. A large-scale commercially produced venison sausage usually contains pork, as the red game meat itself is very lean. Venison can, however, be moistened for sausages with seasonal vegetables and fruits, and brings a much deeper flavour to a casing than the traditional pork. But a good pork sausage, even if seasoned quite plainly with pungent black pepper and maybe a spice like mace, is a triumph if the texture of the meat is right. The mark of a good sausage for me is the need to chew because it has been made with identifiable minced meat and not a slurry of reclaimed protein.

Bill O'Hagan was a roué and a quantifiable risk as a sparring partner for cookery demonstrations, but he was a gourmet and a sausage fanatic who would dream up new flavour combinations almost unceasingly. I cooked his sausages with a rhubarb sauce once – suddenly he was making pork and rhubarb sausages. He would explore numerous sage varieties before opting for a certain one. Savory was a favourite seasoning for him, and beer of course featured in several of his recipes too. Summer shows and events are not the same without him but luckily his rugby loving son Liam is carrying on their business, just one of several fabulous West Sussex sausage producers.

Sausages with Curly Kale and Chestnut Stir-Fry

Serves 3–4

A winter recipe for an easy one-pan supper. I always keep some peeled chestnuts in the freezer at home for dishes like this, but you could use a rinsed and drained can of butter beans in their place if you wish. Always check cooking directions on a sausage pack – if it says they need 20 minutes to cook, amend this recipe accordingly.

1 onion
1 green and 1 red pepper
200g curly kale
4 rashers smoked back bacon
6 large pork sausages
1 tbsp olive oil
200g peeled chestnuts – I prefer frozen, but
vacuum-packed or canned are OK too
1 tbsp fruit or balsamic vinegar

1. Prepare and slice the onion and peppers. Remove any thick stalks from the kale and shred the leaves. Rinse in a colander and shake dry. Cut the bacon into strips – or you could use lardons. (If the kale leaves are large, cook the shreds in boiling water for 1–2 minutes, then

drain before starting the recipe – this removes any bitter flavour.)

2. Snip the sausages apart and cook them in a large non-stick frying pan with the oil for 15 minutes, turning frequently. Remove them from the pan to a plate and cover with a second plate.

3. Add the onion and bacon to the pan juices and stir-fry for 2–3 minutes, until starting to brown. Add the kale, allow it to wilt slightly, then stir-fry for 3–4 minutes, adding the chestnuts as the kale begins to cook down. Slice the sausages thickly.

4. Season the stir-fry to taste with salt and pepper, then return the sausage slices to the pan and cook for 2–3 minutes. Spoon the vinegar into the pan, bubble for a few seconds, season and serve immediately.

Toad in the Hole

Serves 4

A traditional dish that I simply cannot resist. Scrumptious sausages in a crispy batter with homemade chutney. Yes please! I put an onion into my batter for flavour, but it is not essential.

2 large eggs
250g plain flour

300ml milk
1 large onion
25g lard (if possible) or 3 tbsp oil
8 thick sausages

1. Preheat the oven to gas mark 7/220°C. Blend the eggs, flour and milk together with 300ml water to a thick batter, adding some salt and pepper. Leave until required. Finely slice the onion.

2. Heat a suitable roasting tin on the hob, add the lard or oil, then the sausages and cook until they have browned all over. Add the onion about halfway through cooking. Pour the batter into the hot tin and transfer it immediately to the preheated oven.

3. Cook for about 45 minutes, until the batter is crisped and browned. This is great with chutney, onion gravy, homemade ketchup (see page 94) or baked beans.

Venison

We need to eat more of this delicious meat from deer that are thriving in our West Sussex countryside. Venison is lean, full of flavour and utterly delicious. Eating local venison is also a great way to help with conservation as deer are numerous and need regular culling for the preservation of our landscape, and to keep our country roads safe for driving at night.

There are two main species in the county, Fallow and Roe, and they share the same monikers: bucks and does. Bucks may be shot for longer than does, and with Fallow in season from August to April and Roe from April to October, we have a year-round supply of venison. I think Roe is a little sweeter and a real treat.

A glimpse of a deer, especially when in antler, is always special. In Petworth Park the animals are so plentiful that they can often be seen over the estate walls as you drive by. The Petworth herd, established for hunting some

500 years ago, numbers around 900 fallow deer, easily recognisable with off-white spots on their backs and a marked stripe on their tails. Their coats change from a rich chestnut-brown to a grey-brown in the winter, when the spots fade slightly.

Many people think that venison must be marinated for a long time before cooking. I feel this is only necessary if you think your meat is from an older animal. Venison livers are delicious and just as much if not more of a gastro-treat than calf's liver. A venison fillet steak is my idea of meat heaven! However, the most common way of cooking this lean red meat is in casseroles. The forequarter, if diced or minced, can be used for sausages, burgers or stews, leaving the loin fillet and the haunch for roasts. The haunch, or leg, has massive muscles in it and I think that it should be slow roasted for best results, with a good coating of fatty pork for moisture (which maybe counteracts the benefits of the lean meat). I usually cut my haunches in half, and bone the lower leg, cutting some steaks which will pan-fry well, and some casserole dice from the portion not to be roasted.

Venison Steaks with Spiced Chocolate Oil and Apples

Serves 4

This recipe was inspired by my friend Maria Elia, one of the most exciting chefs that I know. We just love talking about and eating food together! Any leftover chocolate oil will keep in the fridge and can be added to casseroles or sauces, or spooned over grilled or pan-fried meats.

For the spiced chocolate oil:

200ml groundnut oil
50g dark chocolate, 70 per cent cocoa
5cm cinnamon stick
1 tsp ground Szechwan peppercorns
1 pinch ground cloves
1 pinch curry powder

For the venison:

2 Bramley apples
A knob of butter
Sugar to taste
4 venison steaks
1 tbsp olive oil

1. Heat all the ingredients for the spiced chocolate oil together until the chocolate is melted. Whisk into an emulsion, then season to taste with salt and pepper. Keep warm until required.

2. Peel, core and finely slice the apple into a pan and cook quickly with 1–2 tbsp water until soft. Add a knob of butter and sugar to taste and keep warm.

3. Season the venison with ground black pepper. Heat a frying pan until hot, then add the oil and the venison steaks. Cook as directed or for 3–4 minutes on each side. Allow to rest for at least 5 minutes in the pan.

4. Serve the venison on a splodge of the cooked apple, with a generous amount of chocolate oil spooned over the meat, and with vegetables or salad of your choice. I love watercress with this. Remoulade is good too, traditionally raw celeriac but turnip works well, coarsely grated into a mustard and/or garlic mayonnaise with chopped walnuts.

Italian-Style Venison or Hare Casserole, or Pasta Ragoût

Serves 4

The unusual thing about this recipe is the use of white wine with red meat, which is very Italian. Hare also makes a fabulous game ragoût for pasta when cooked in this way.

1 onion
1 large carrot
2 sticks celery
1 clove garlic
4 rashers smoked streaky bacon
1 tbsp olive oil
750g diced stewing venison, boned out hare or
a mix of both
1 tsp dried oregano
3 bay leaves
350ml dry white wine
2 tbsp tomato purée
50g toasted pine nuts
50g raisins
25g dark bitter chocolate
Chopped parsley to garnish

1. Preheat the oven to gas mark 3/160°C. Prepare the vegetables, finely chopping the onion, carrot, celery and garlic. Chop the bacon too.
2. Heat the oil in a flameproof casserole, add the onion, carrot, celery and bacon, cover and cook slowly for 5–6 minutes, stirring once. Add the meat and herbs and cook for a further 2–3 minutes, then add the wine, tomato purée and seasonings, and a little water or

stock, if necessary, to cover the meat. Bring to the boil, cover and cook in the oven for 3 hours.

3. Return the casserole to the hob and add the pine nuts, raisins and chocolate, stirring until the chocolate has melted. Season to taste with extra salt and pepper, then garnish with parsley before serving with vegetables, or as a rich and unusual sauce for pasta.

Knepp Castle Wildland Project

When I owned my deli in Arundel in the early 1980s, I stocked ice creams from Knepp Castle, and I know that my major competitor, Harrods of Knightsbridge, did too! It was delicious ice cream but, sadly, is now a thing of the past, as the dairy herd was deemed unviable and the estate looked elsewhere for agricultural activities to maintain their historic lands and home.

Imagine my surprise when in July 2013 I was looking for something to eat at the Rolling Stones farewell concert in Hyde Park, only to find Garlic Wood Farm offering Knepp Castle meat, sizzling and appetising, on a barbecue stand. Local food follows me around these days!

Knepp is turning back the clock and letting its land go native again. I first heard about the scheme on the same BBC *Countryfile* programme that I shamelessly flirted my way through whilst cooking pumpkins with Matt Baker! No more straightening of river courses for the Burrells on their land. The estate is grazed by two groups of animals: Roe deer and rabbits, which came uninvited, and Old English Longhorn cattle, Tamworth pigs, Fallow deer and Exmoor ponies, all of which the estate has introduced as the prime grazers, first in the park and now on the wider estate. By taking the land out of cereal production, running the stock on it and then letting the area regenerate naturally, it is hoped that the increased natural fertility and general lushness of growth will suit the animals well. It should allow them to breed well and, for those that we eat, to supply top-class meat. Each table breed has been selected for the quality and taste of its meat, and the work involved in grazing for the animals will ensure slower growth and therefore good in-muscle marbling and eating quality. A survey to assess ten years of the Wildland Project is due to take place in 2015.

A project like this could only ever be undertaken on a progressive family estate. Through Knepp's association with Garlic Wood Farm and events held on the estate, more and more people are having the opportunity to taste the wonderful difference that natural grazing, rich in wild flowers and plants, makes to the meat. And naturalists must love the project too – Knepp is often tweeting about rare insects, flora and fauna seen on the estate.

So, back to Garlic Wood Farm, Hyde Park and the Rolling Stones. We came across the Knepp meat on the Garlic Wood Farm stand simply because we had gone to the concert well, only partly to hear the Stones. They had selected The 1975 as one of their support acts and we have known their drummer since birth – I used to share a cottage with his mum. Their best-known song? 'Chocolate', of course.

Drinks

Beer and Ale

I love beer! The ever-growing number of microbreweries around our county is a drinker's delight. The only frustration for me is in wondering why so many pubs still stick to the ubiquitous range of pumps dispensing lagers and big brands when there is so much craft ale of real character being brewed around West Sussex.

I want to tackle the difference between beers, ales and lagers, which might be pedantic but often causes confusion. Beer is an umbrella term for drinks made from water, malt, hops and yeast, the malt coming from barley. How the malt is roasted and the choice of hops that are used (and sometimes when they are added) defines the flavour of the finished beer. There are two types of beers: ales and lagers.

Lagers are generally lighter in colour and are made with yeast that works best at cool temperatures. Ales have a huge range of styles, colours and flavours, are fermented at a higher temperature and usually drunk at room temperature or only slightly chilled. Most people like their lagers cold. The exception to the rule for ales might be stout, which is delicious really cold with shellfish.

I went to a fascinating tasting once where a much-loved beer of 5 per cent ABV was tasted against a 3.4 per cent ABV version, in an attempt to see if a lower-alcohol brew might become a success as a pub-session beer. The result was like dating a teenager instead of a man! All the characteristics were there, but none of the body. Craft beers are not for glugging: they are for savouring and drinking more slowly.

We really do love beer at home and quite often give supper parties matching a different beer to each course. It is fun to do and I generally cook with the same beer that we drink.

It is worth searching through junk shops and vintage stalls for unusual glasses to enjoy your beer from. Stemmed, squat, curvaceous or a tumbler, the shape of your glass adds to the enjoyment of your beer, with darker ales keeping the secrets of their complex flavours better in a tall, thin glass, whereas light, bright beers sparkle in wider glasses; a Babycham glass is great!

Beer-Soaked Brisket

Serves 4

Choose a spicy ale for this pot roast, a winter or brown ale. Dark Star's The Art of Darkness would be good, or Old Knucker from Arundel Brewery.

2–3 onions
2–3 carrots
2 tbsp olive oil
1kg boned and rolled brisket of beef
500ml bottle of ale

1. Choose a saucepan or a flameproof casserole that the beef will fit into snugly, and which has a tightly fitting lid. Prepare the vegetables and chop them into chunks.

2. Heat the oil in the selected pan, then add the brisket and brown it on all sides. Pack the vegetables around the joint then add sufficient beer to come about halfway up the beef. Bring to the boil, then cover the pan and simmer very slowly for 3–4 hours, turning the beef once or twice during that time.

3. Let the beef stand for 10 minutes or so in the beer before carving. Season the beer juices as gravy and serve the vegetables too, if you wish. Serve with roast or baked potatoes and/or Yorkshire pudding.

Stout Cake

Makes 1 large cake

This really needs to be kept for a few days before eating – but it never is in our house!

500ml bottle stout of your choice
350g mixed cake fruit
3 large eggs
150g butter, at room temperature, or chilled
soft baking margarine
150g light muscovado sugar
250g self-raising flour
1 tsp baking powder
2–3 tbsp marmalade
25g toasted flaked almonds

1. Open the beer, pour half into a glass and drink it whilst making the cake. Soak the fruit in a bowl in 150ml of the remaining beer.

2. Preheat the oven to gas mark 3/160°C. Lightly butter a large loaf tin (19cm x 9cm x 6cm) and cut a piece of baking parchment or an old butter paper to line the base of the tin. You can get paper cake-tin liners for this size tin, which are ideal.

3. Break the eggs into a mixing bowl and beat them together with a fork. Add the softened butter, sugar, flour and baking powder, then beat the whole lot together with a wooden spoon until blended, then

231

continue beating for 1 minute. Do this in a mixer if you have one, but a bowl and spoon is much better aerobic exercise!

4. Beat the fruit and its beer into the mixture, then pile it into the prepared tin. Make a dip down the centre of the mixture, then bake immediately in the preheated oven for 1½ hours.

5. Allow the cake to cool slightly in the tin, then turn it out and cool completely on a wire rack. Make skewer holes all over the top of the cake, right through, then gradually pour in the remaining beer.

6. Heat the marmalade until it melts, then brush it over the top of the cake, or spread it. Scatter the toasted almonds over the marmalade so that they stick to the cake.

7. Now, this is the difficult part. Wrap the cake in baking parchment and then foil and leave well alone for 2–3 days before eating, to allow the cake to mature. This is hard but worth it!

Cider, Apple and Pear Juices

Cider is one of the trendiest of drinks and yet the 'session' ciders and perries (for perry it is if made of pear juice) that have driven the revival bear little resemblance in taste to craft drinks, which really showcase the fruit. The traditional making of juices, for fermented or non-fermented drinks, is very simple. The fruit is crushed, then layered up in sacking or webbing, sometimes on pallet-like boards, until there is a whole stack of these 'cheeses'. Then pressure is applied, usually on a screw-down press, until all the juice has been squeezed from the fruit and collected. Some processors will press one variety of juice at a time and then blend the varieties to taste. Others, especially cider-makers, who know the fruit balance for their recipe, might press a number of fruit varieties in the right proportions for their craft drink. The delight of an artisan product is that it might vary just a little from year to year, making vintages stand out from each other.

Cider comes in many forms, from rough and scrumpy-like to elegantly dry and sparkling. There's a time and an occasion for all types of this delicious drink. Apple or pear juice made from fruit and not from concentrate is full of flavour, and has a thickness of texture that makes it special to drink, and also to cook with. The advantage of cooking with cider or fruit juice is that the acidity in the drink will act as a seasoning for the other ingredients in the dish, sharpening their flavours (which is what acidity brings to your cooking) and therefore cutting down on the amount of salt, pepper or sugar required to finally season the dish.

◇————◇•◇————◇

Mussels with Cider and Apple

Serves 2

This could be made with apple juice instead of cider if you prefer. The apple with the mussels is delicious.

1kg mussels
1 medium onion
1 clove garlic

Small bunch of parsley
1 eating apple
1 tbsp olive oil
2 bay leaves
350ml cider

1. Empty the mussels into a sink of cold water. Pull off any beards (rope-like bits sticking out of the side of the shells) and scrape the shells clean of any barnacles. Discard any mussels that do not close when tapped on the side of the sink. Drain in a colander.

2. Finely chop the onion, peel the garlic, finely chop the parsley and finely dice the eating apple, leaving the skin on.

3. Heat the oil in a large saucepan, add the onion with the bay leaves and cook slowly for 5 minutes until soft. Crush the garlic into the pan, add the apple and cider and bring quickly to the boil.

4. Tip the mussels into the pan, cover and cook quickly for 3–4 minutes, until all the shells have opened. Shake the pan vigorously once or twice during cooking. Scoop the mussels into a bowl with a slotted spoon, season the liquor to taste and add the parsley. Pour over the mussels and serve with crusty bread to mop up the juices.

Apple or Cider Cake

Makes 18 pieces

You can use either juice or cider for this deliciously moist tray bake, which will keep the family, or the office, happy. You could serve it warm, with custard. Home comforts.

1 crisp eating apple
Juice of ½ a lemon
3 large eggs
350g self-raising flour
1 tsp bicarbonate of soda
1 tsp ground cinnamon
175g soft baking margarine
175g caster sugar
275ml apple juice or cider

1. Preheat the oven to gas mark 4/180°C. Line a tin (about 20 x 30cm) with baking parchment. Quarter and core the apple, then slice it finely into the lemon juice and toss to prevent the slices from browning. Whether or not you leave the skin on the apple is up to you.

2. Beat the eggs in a large bowl, then add the flour, bicarbonate of soda, cinnamon, sugar and margarine. Beat well until blended, then beat for a further 30 seconds. Gradually add the apple juice or cider, beating all the time, then turn the mixture into the prepared tin and level the top.

3. Decorate with the apple slices then bake for about 1 hour, until the cake springs back when touched and a skewer inserted into the centre comes out clean. Sprinkle with more sugar then leave in the tin for 5–10 minutes before lifting out on to a wire rack to cool completely. Cut into 18 pieces.

Coffee

We live in a coffee-culture society – pretty much as our forefathers did in the late seventeenth century. Business and coffee have been indivisible ever since. Coffee, coffee breaks, coffee machines, coffee culture: people don't expect to go to work and not be able to have a caffeine-rich drink to keep them on their toes. There are now many coffee roasters throughout the area, and community shops, restaurants and other outlets often have their own blend supplied by a local coffee company. The beans themselves keep for years in their green state – that is, until they are roasted. The higher the roast, the stronger or richer the flavour and the darker the colour of the bean.

Cooking with coffee is a real challenge: to make a great coffee ice cream requires a lot of skill as freezing can accentuate bitterness, and so the correct amount of sugar and spice must be used to enhance, support and deepen the coffee flavour without over-sweetening. Coffee in chocolate has been done brilliantly by Montezuma's, in both bars and drinking chocolate flakes.

Coffee and Walnut Ice Cream

Serves 6–8

There was a performance of Bach's 'Coffee Cantata' at the East Beach Café in Littlehampton – it was great and my first introduction to the quirky work. It inspired this, the best recipe that I have ever written for coffee ice cream. The cream measures are approximate as pot sizes change so much. Approximate is fine.

300ml single cream (approx.)
100ml freshly made espresso (a double shot)
Pinch mixed spice
4 large egg yolks
75g Demerara sugar
100g caster sugar
50g walnuts, chopped or broken
300ml whipping cream (approx.)

1. Heat the double cream, coffee and spice until almost boiling.

2. Beat the egg yolks with the brown sugar until pale and thick while the cream is heating, then pour on the coffee cream, stirring continuously.

3. Rinse the pan in cold water, then return the mixture to it and heat gently, stirring all the time, just until the cream is thick enough to coat the back of a wooden spoon. Allow to cool completely and chill for an hour.

4. Prepare the caramelised nuts. Heat the caster sugar gently until melted then bring to the boil and cook until golden brown. Add the walnuts, shaking them until coated, then tip the mixture on to a lightly oiled baking sheet. Leave until completely cold and hard, then chop roughly.

5. Add the whipping cream to the coffee custard, then turn into an ice cream machine and freeze-churn until very thick. Add the caramelised walnuts and continue churning until they are evenly distributed throughout and the ice cream is ready for serving. Alternatively, freeze in a suitable container for 4–5 hours, stirring 2 or 3 times and adding the nuts as the mixture starts to thicken. Whisk the whipping cream until thick before folding it into the coffee custard if you do not have an ice cream machine.

Ginger and Coffee Creams

Makes about 20

I love the flavours of ginger and coffee together, and the combination in a biscuit to dunk is doubly delicious.

200g plain flour
2 tsp baking powder
1 tsp bicarbonate of soda
2 tsp ground ginger
1 tsp mixed spice
25g caster sugar
100g butter
150g golden syrup

For the icing:

50g butter at room temperature
50g caster sugar
1 tsp coffee essence
75g icing sugar

1. Preheat the oven to gas mark 5/190°C. Butter 2 or 3 baking sheets.

2. Sieve all flour, raising agents and spices together into a bowl, stir in the sugar and make a well in the centre. Heat the butter and syrup in a small pan until the

241

butter has melted, then pour it into the flour and mix into a dough – it will be soft but not sticky.

3. Roll generous half teaspoons of the mix into balls, place them on the baking sheets, quite well apart to allow for spreading, then flatten them just a little with the back of a spoon. Bake for 15–20 minutes, until set. Leave for a few minutes before transferring to a wire rack to cool completely.

4. Make the icing by beating the butter, caster sugar and coffee together and then gradually adding the icing sugar, which should be sieved into the mixture. Sandwich pairs of biscuits together with the icing and some restraint – otherwise too much icing will squidge out when you bite the biscuits.

5. Store these in a tin. They will soften slightly once iced, but they keep well for 2–3 days.

Wine

The toast of the county! And indeed, in some cases, of the world! West Sussex is capitalising on its greensand terroir and planting vines almost right across the county for the production of sparkling and table wines. These wines are ageing into maturity and the bubbly ones are giving many Champagnes a slightly flat feeling.

The combination of grape juices needed for the fermentation of wines in the classic Champagne-style (one has to be very careful of terminology here) is from Pinot Noir, Pinot Meunier, and Chardonnay. Obviously the growing of the red grape varieties had to be right before any serious thought could be given to producing dry sparkling wines. The pioneers were Nyetimber from their home vineyards at Pulborough, but now their production is expanding and the public can easily see some of their newer vines around the splendid Roman villa at Bignor. Ridgeview vineyard near Ditchling has always used the term Cuvée Merret on their bottles. This honours Christopher Merret, a seventeenth-century wine buff, who presented a paper explaining the process for making sparkling wine to the Royal Society 30 years before said process was documented in France. Sparkling wine is one of the fastest-growing and most exciting areas of artisan production in our county, as smaller vineyards bring their own characterful and delicious wines to our notice.

I am not going to suggest that you cook with West Sussex sparkling wines: that would be too decadent! However, I have long been a fan of blue cheese with sparkling wine and wholeheartedly recommend Molecombe Blue on melba toasts when you next open a bottle of local bubbles.

There is a long history of winemaking in West Sussex and the new generation of table wine producers are successfully carrying on a tradition for a public now more ready to celebrate English wines. One of the oldest vineyards is Bolney Estate, which celebrated its 40th anniversary in 2013. Bolney's Pinot Noir was the first local red wine I tasted that I thought 'had legs' or would make a go of it and, indeed, the vineyard has won many awards. Like all Pinots, it is fine with lamb and mutton, with its complex fruity flavour matching the rich, grassiness of our local meat very well.

Daube of Beef

Serves 6

I like to use shin of beef for this, and to cook it for as long as possible. There is always the debate as to whether casseroles are better reheated the next day, but this one is full of flavour fresh from the oven.

1 large onion
3 large carrots
3 sticks celery
6 rashers streaky bacon
1 orange
3 tbsp olive oil
6 thick slices of shin of beef, about 1kg
1 tbsp fresh thyme leaves, or 1 tsp dried
1 large cinnamon stick
2 bay leaves
1 bottle (75cl) full-bodied red wine
2 tbsp tapenade (black olive paste)
Freshly chopped parsley

1. Preheat the oven to gas mark 3/160°C. Finely dice the onion, carrots, celery and bacon to the same size. Peel the zest from the orange in large, fine strips. Squeeze the juice and reserve it.

2. Heat a large flameproof casserole, add the oil then add the meat, half at a time, and brown it on both sides. Remove to a plate and add a little more oil if necessary

to brown the second batch. Do this in batches so that you do brown the meat and do not steam it as the pan cools and juices flow. Add the dicd veg and bacon to the meat juices in the pan, stir, cover and reduce the heat. Cook slowly for 10 minutes, stirring once or twice.

3. Return the beef to the pan with the orange zest, aromatic seasonings, and some salt and pepper. Pour in the wine and bring to a slow boil. Cover and transfer to a slow oven for at least 3 hours, or longer of you wish.

4. Remove the beef to a plate and keep it warm. Boil the wine mix to reduce it to a thicker sauce, if necessary, then remove the orange zest. Stir in the tapenade and taste before adjusting the seasonings and returning the meat to the pan. I like to serve this with tagliatelle tossed in melted butter, the reserved orange juice and chopped parsley.

Oxtail Ragoût

Serves 3–4

This is a recipe to make at the weekend – it is cooked in two long sessions, which could be over two days, has quite a few ingredients and just takes too long to contemplate at the end of a normal working day. It is, however, quite simply sublime – surprisingly light but full of complex flavours.

Stage 1
1 large onion
1 stick celery
1 carrot
600–700g oxtail, cut into joints
2 tbsp olive oil
2 bay leaves and 1 cinnamon stick

Stage 2
2 sticks celery
1 medium leek
1 medium carrot
100g smoked bacon

Stage 3
1 red chilli, seeded and finely chopped
2 tbsp olive oil
1 tbsp fresh thyme leaves or 1 tsp dried thyme
250ml dry white wine
1 tbsp tomato purée
25g dark bitter chocolate, 70 per cent cocoa
Raisins and pine nuts
Freshly chopped parsley
Freshly cooked pasta to serve – I suggest
pappardelle or tagliatelle

1. Preheat the oven to gas mark 3/160°C. Scrub but do
not peel the onion, celery and carrot, then chop them
roughly. The skins will help the stock. Season the
oxtail well with salt and pepper. Heat a small covered

247

casserole that will just take the meat, add the oil, then brown half the oxtail pieces all over, over a moderately high heat – not too fierce or the meat will just burn. Repeat with the remaining pieces.

2. Put all the oxtail back in the pan, add the chopped veg and seasonings, and sufficient water to cover the ingredients. Bring to the boil, then skim any sediment from the surface of the pan. Cover and cook slowly for about 3 hours in the preheated oven, or on the floor of the Aga simmering oven.

3. Remove the oxtail from the casserole, and pour everything else through a sieve, catching the liquor. Discard the spent vegetables. Take the meat from the oxtail, discarding the bones, and any of the fatty membrane around the meat.

4. Prepare and chop the remaining celery, leek and carrot, and the bacon. Seed and finely chop the chilli.

5. Heat a fresh saucepan, add the remaining olive oil and the chopped leek, celery, carrot and chilli with the thyme, cover and cook slowly for about 10 minutes, stirring several times. Add the oxtail with the white wine, some seasoning and the tomato purée, and a little reserved liquor, if necessary, to cover. Bring slowly to the boil, cover and simmer or cook again in your slow oven. How long you cook the ragoût for at this stage is pretty much up to you, but a minimum of 1 hour if you simmer it and 2–3 hours in the oven. Basically, the longer the better in terms of achieving the best blend of

flavours. If you simmer the sauce you may need to top up the pan with a little more of the oxtail liquor from time to time.

6. Cook your chosen pasta as directed. Meanwhile, toast the pine nuts in a dry frying pan, then add them to the ragoût with the raisins and finely chopped chocolate. Stir until the chocolate has melted (just watch the sauce darken!) then season to taste with salt and freshly ground black pepper. Add chopped parsley, then toss the sauce through the drained pasta and serve immediately.

Store-
Cupboard
Essentials

Chocolate

Not really a store-cupboard ingredient, more a way of life! And yet I do use chocolate a lot in my cooking and we do have some fabulous chocolatiers in West Sussex. Grown here? No, but certainly we are developing a reputation as a county producing fine chocolates, one of the fastest-growing sectors of the grocery market today. Everyone needs (and wants) a treat!

Chocolate is a passion and it is about passion. It is the only food that melts at blood heat, hence the sensuous reputation that goes with it. The thickness of the confection doesn't actually alter its taste, but it does affect how you receive the flavour: if too thick it takes too long for all the components of the chocolate to make an impression on your senses together as it melts on your tongue. This leads to disappointment – something which should never be the outcome of eating the confectionery. The purer the chocolate, the more complex the flavour.

251

Enjoy slowly and you might taste berry fruits, stone fruits, earthy cherries, tobacco, vanilla, caramel: many of these tastes come from the terroir of the cocoa, the characteristics of the land on which it was grown, as well as the processing.

It is worth remembering that cocoa is savoury more than sweet, and that the chocolate drink of Montezuma's era was very different indeed to the modern hot chocolate. Cocoa, like so many of our foods, originates from Mexico and Montezuma was the original pin-up of the chocolate-eating heart-throbs. Both Mayans and Aztecs appear to have been addicted to their cocoa drinks, often flavoured with chillies, by the end of the first millennium. What goes around comes around!

West Sussex chocolate makers now revisit the most original of seasonings as they create chilli chocolate extravaganzas each year for the West Dean Chilli Fiesta. These are part and parcel of our county's gastro identity now, but it is the new style of cocoa-rich dark milk chocolates, along with the bean-to-bar selection, that really excites my taste buds. Frequently.

Earl Grey and Milk Chocolate Mousse

Serves 6

This is a wonderful way of lightening the flavour of a rich dessert: the bergamot in the Earl Grey is perfect with Montezuma's Dark Side milk chocolate.

(Please note: this recipe contains raw egg.)

4 strong Earl Grey teabags
200g dark milk chocolate
2 large eggs
150ml double cream
Extra cream and chocolate flake to decorate

1. Place the teabags in a measuring jug and add boiling water to 100ml. Leave for 5 minutes, then remove the bags and leave the tea to cool slightly.

2. Break the chocolate into squares, place it in a large bowl over hot water and heat gently until the chocolate has melted. Don't let the water boil as steam getting into the chocolate will affect its texture and cannot be rectified – just have the pan on a very low heat. Remove the bowl and beat the chocolate until smooth, then leave to cool for a few minutes.

3. Meanwhile, separate the eggs, adding the yolks to the chocolate and placing the whites in a clean bowl. Whisk

the whites until stiff – they should stay firm in the bowl when you tip it upside down. Whisk the cream until thick and floppy.

4. Beat the egg yolks and the tea into the chocolate – as they combine the chocolate will become darker and glossy. Using a wire whisk, combine the cream into the chocolate with gentle figure-of-eight strokes, then finally add the egg whites, half at a time, and combine in the same way. Do not beat the mousse or you will knock out the air and make it heavy.

5. Chill for at least 2 hours, then decorate with more whipped cream if you wish, and shaved chocolate or crushed chocolate flake. The tea flavour becomes stronger if you can leave the mousses for 6–8 hours before serving.

Chilli Con Carne

Serves 4

Back to the very roots of chocolate: Mexico. Here I use it to season the chilli meat sauce at the end of cooking.

1 large onion
1 green chilli
1 clove garlic
1 tbsp oil
500g lean minced beef

1 tbsp chilli powder
2 tbsp wine vinegar
400g can chopped tomatoes
2 tbsp tomato purée
410g can kidney beans
50g dark bitter chocolate

1. Prepare the vegetables, then chop the onion, and seed and finely chop the chilli with the garlic. Heat the oil in a pan, add the vegetables and cook slowly for 5 minutes. Add the beef and chilli powder, increase the heat and cook until well browned.

2. Pull off the heat, add the vinegar, chopped tomatoes and tomato purée and some salt, then bring to the boil and simmer for 30 minutes, or longer if you have time.

3. Drain and rinse the kidney beans, add them to the chilli and continue cooking for a further 10 minutes, uncovered. Stir the chocolate, broken into squares, into the chilli then taste it before adding extra seasoning. Serve with rice, or in baked potatoes with guacamole and salad.

Flour

Most people don't give flour a second thought – it's just there in the cupboard when you need it. It is when you get interested in bread making that curiosity about varieties of wheat and their relative protein values take over. The minute you know you are after a 12–13 per cent protein content for your daily loaves you start looking at flour packs with greater interest. Bread can, however, be made with any protein content above 10 per cent. The lower the protein, the lower the rise.

Bread flour is best milled in the traditional way, using grinding stones and not metal rollers. Stone grinding produces a rounder flavour in my opinion, and that is exactly the style of milling for our most local of flours, produced at the Weald & Downland Open Air Museum at Singleton near Chichester, where the mill is well worth a visit. Bread flour is milled from hard wheat, the same style of wheat that is used to make pasta. This is obtained in the main from spring wheat. Wholewheat flour uses every part of the grain, whereas brown flour is usually just around 85 per cent after the bran has been removed for other products. I mix about ⅔ wholewheat to ⅓ white. This provides a density of crumb that is a pleasure to eat and is not too worthy and heavy. Bread making and eating is all about pleasure for me.

We are experimenting with sourdoughs at home, which I have to say are trickier than you might imagine: you have to keep your starter in good condition and the dough is generally wetter than others, and trickier to handle, but my recipe is working well for us. The flavour is, well, sour, but great with cheese, cold meats or marmalade; sourdough toast is delicious.

The following two recipes constituted a one-hour cookery demonstration as an introduction to bread making. Of course there was a great deal of *Blue Peter*-style preparation but people left determined to try the recipes at home. I hope that you will too – it's a very different method of making bread. If bread making is not for you there are now many fabulous artisan bakers around the county producing sourdoughs, traditional loaves and all-too-tempting cakes. Happiness is good baking!

The Moon's New Wholewheat Bread

Makes 2 family-sized loaves

This is lightly yeasted and starts with a flying ferment, a bubble of yeast and floury water, which concentrates the flavour of the finished loaf.

850ml tepid water
7g sachet fast-action dried yeast
900g wholewheat flour
1 tbsp fine sea salt
3 tbsp olive oil
400g strong white bread flour

1. Measure the water into a large mixing bowl, then stir in the yeast and 500g of wholewheat flour. This will give a thick liquid of about the same consistency as unwhipped cream or natural yogurt. Cover the bowl with cling film or a warm damp tea towel and leave for 15–20 minutes.

2. The liquid should be starting to ferment or bubble (this is called a flying ferment) – it won't be dramatic but there should be bubbles on the surface. If not, leave for a further 10 minutes.

3. Stir in the salt and olive oil with the white flour and the remaining wholewheat. Mix it in the bowl, first with a wooden spoon and then with your hand, to a

manageable but slightly soft dough. Damp your hand as you mix with extra water if it is too dry.

4. Punch the dough down in the bowl, then fold the dough in from the edge to the centre, turn the bowl ¼ turn and repeat until you have folded the dough 10 times. Cover the bowl and leave for 10 minutes.

5. Repeat step four above three times, until the dough has had four kneadings. You will feel it changing as you knead it. Cover again and leave for 1 hour after the fourth knead.

6. Punch the dough down again gently in the bowl, then turn it on to a lightly floured work surface and divide it into two (even after more than 30 years of bread making we don't always get this perfectly even) and shape it to go into two large 900g oiled loaf tins. The most professional loaves have the dough slightly rolled so that you see a spiral in the ends of the baked loaves.

7. Cover with the damp towel again and leave for about 45 minutes until well risen. Sprinkle a little extra flour over the risen dough.

8. To bake. For a gas or electric oven, place the bread on a shelf just below the centre in a COLD oven. Set the temperature to gas mark 7/220°C and bake for 45 minutes. Turn the loaves out of the tins and tap the bases – if they sound hollow the bread is cooked. If not, pop the loaves back into the oven, not in the tins and just on the shelf, for a further 5 minutes or so. In an Aga, place a wire shelf on the floor of the roasting oven and

then bake the loaves for 25 minutes. Insert the cold shelf (which should be cold and not stored in the Aga!) on the top set of runners and bake for a further 20 minutes.

9. Turn the bread out of the tins and cool on a wire rack. Aga owners – remember to remove the cold shelf and cool it down again. Keep tins just for bread and do not wash them – the high heat and a little oil each time you bake will season the surface and make them ideal for bread.

Basic White Sourdough

Makes 1 large loaf

As this is not a speciality bread book I suggest that you acquire some sourdough starter. Check feastofwestsussex. co.uk for more details of starting your own. Liquid and weight measures are interchangeable.

500g strong white bread flour
10g/2 tsp fine sea salt
300g/ml warm water
150g white sourdough starter (made 6–8 hours
in advance with 8g starter, 80g white bread flour
and 80g/ml water. There will be a little over to feed
for your next starter.)

1. Mix the flour and salt in one bowl, and the starter and water (ideally at about 30°C) in another. Pour the flour into the liquid, mix until coming together with a wooden spoon, then pull together into a dough with your hand. It may be slightly sticky but don't be tempted to add more flour. If very sticky just flour your hand, then knead the dough in the bowl by folding it in on itself and pressing down, then turning the bowl ¼ turn in front of you. Do this 10 times: fold, press, turn; fold, press, turn. The dough will start to change under your hands. Cover with the other bowl and leave for 10 minutes.

2. Press the dough out flat in the base of the bowl. If it is sticky put just a little flour onto the back of your knuckles then fold, press and turn as above another 10 times. Cover and leave for 10 minutes.

3. Repeat until the dough has been kneaded 4 times, then cover and leave for 1 hour.

4. Knead again and then shape the dough for the mega-proving. If you have a woven sourdough basket, flour it very well – really, very well, with a little flour lying in the base – then make the dough into the appropriate shape and set it into the floured basket. If you don't have a basket, flour a clean tea towel thoroughly then use it to line a colander or suitable shallow bowl, and shape the dough to set into that. Do make sure that there is enough flour on the towel though to stop the loaf from sticking (yes, this is more complicated than baking in tins).

5. Cover and leave for 4–6 hours or longer, until well risen – I cover it with a supermarket bag for life, pulled up well off the surface of the dough. By the side of the Aga it works a treat. If you are a light sleeper or don't sleep much you can time your making and baking so that this goes on overnight. You can also do the proving in the fridge overnight – experiment, but give the dough an hour to come back to room temperature before baking.

6. Now, the tricky bit. Preheat the oven to gas mark 7/220°C. Flour a baking sheet or line it with baking parchment. Turn the sourdough out onto the baking sheet – hence the need for all that flour. Brush away the excess with a pastry brush, then bake in the hot oven for about 30 minutes. If you like a crispy crust, set a roasting tin with 200ml water in the bottom of the oven.

7. Check the bread is baked by tapping the base – it should sound hollow so pop it back for a few minutes if it doesn't. Then cool the loaf on a wire rack and feast once chronic indigestion from very hot bread is no longer a possibility/probability!

Honey

Bee warned! West Sussex is a-buzz with honey. So much of the county is good agricultural land in the highest stewardship campaigns. This means wide field margins and plenty of wild flowers on which the bees can feast, whilst helping out with pollination. Commercial courgette fields, inter-planted with wild-flower strips, are a sight to salivate over, whether you are human or *Apis Apini*, the Honey bee.

Paynes Southdown Bee Farms are a third-generation family business based in Hassocks. They gather honey from hives positioned all along the Downs, selling through local shops and tourist attractions. When I had a deli in Arundel they were one of my most welcomed suppliers – their products just flew off the shelves. Paynes also realises how many people like to keep bees at home, and shares knowledge through the produce and equipment shop on its site in Hassocks.

Most amateur beekeepers only have two or three hives and many join a local association for help, advice and access to reasonably priced supplies. West Sussex Beekeepers' Association developed from a group based in the Midhurst and Chichester area and, established in 1941, it now has over 400 members which shows the popularity of beekeeping at home. I was lent some beekeeping equipment by a member in North Mundham to prop a photo for my very first cookbook, published well over 25 years ago! I have always loved cooking with honey.

Honey was around to sweeten our West Sussex cooking long before sugar. It adds a depth of flavour unachievable with other sweeteners but, like sea salt crystals, needs time to dissolve into dishes to change the flavour. Add honey and taste within a few seconds and the magic will not have happened. Leave it for 2–3 minutes before making your decision about seasoning some more. If you ever have the chance to taste some single-origin honeys, for example, lime blossom or bay, do try them as they have quite different flavours, as does heather honey from Scotland.

Slow-Roast Shoulder of Southdown Lamb with Honeyed Root Vegetables

Serves 4–6

Shoulder is my favourite joint of lamb. It has a naturally sweet flavour and is really good value, in truth because it has big bones which make carving difficult. No worries though in this easy, all-in-one roast, where the meat is cooked so that it just falls off the bone. You can use whatever root vegetables are your favourites – parsnips, onions or carrots could easily be used in place of any of the veg suggested here. I add honey as a glaze to the vegetables while the lamb is resting, which makes the most of its delicious flavour.

1 large sweet potato
1 small butternut squash
2 bulbs fennel
12 shallots
2 tbsp oil
1½kg shoulder of lamb
3 tbsp honey
Freshly chopped parsley to garnish

1. Preheat the oven to gas mark 6/200°C. Choose a large roasting tin or flat casserole and place it in the oven while it is heating up.

2. Prepare the vegetables, then chop the sweet potato and squash into 1½cm chunks, thickly slice the fennel and leave the shallots whole.

3. Pour the oil into the roasting tin, then add the vegetables, season them well and turn them in the oil.

4. Rub some salt and pepper all over the lamb. Snuggle the meat on top of the vegetables and roast in the hot oven for 1 hour.

5. Reduce the heat to gas mark 4/180°C, cover with a lid or foil and continue roasting for a further 2 hours. You can turn the heat down lower and leave it for longer if you are going out.

6. Leave the meat to stand on a warm plate, covered, for 10 minutes. Spoon the honey over the vegetables then turn them carefully to coat them with the now honeyed meat juices. Return the vegetables to the oven. Pull the meat away from the bones in large pieces using 2 forks – this is much easier than carving! Pile the honey-glazed vegetables and meat onto warm plates, garnish with chopped parsley and serve immediately.

Honeyed Pork and Apple Tortillas

Serves 4

The home of Old El Paso products used to be in Chichester, so I think of tortillas as local food! They make fabulous family fare and the honey in this stir-fry is most unusual.

1 pork tenderloin fillet, about 350–400g
1 leek
2 sticks celery
2 eating apples
2 tbsp groundnut oil
Good pinch chilli flakes
1–2 tbsp honey
4 large flour tortillas
200g tub hummus

1. Trim the pork and cut it into 6 mm slices. Trim, prepare and slice the leek and celery, then finely dice the apples.

2. Heat a large frying pan or wok, add the oil then the pork and stir-fry quickly until starting to brown on all sides. Add the celery with the chilli flakes and most of the apple and cook for a further 1–2 minutes, then stir in the honey to taste. Season with salt and pepper.

3. Spread the tortillas with a little hummus, then top with the pork. Scatter the remaining apple over, then roll up and eat immediately. You can heat the tortillas before filling them if you wish, according to the instructions on the packet.

Oils

Oil has become an indispensable ingredient in the modern store cupboard, even though it was virtually unknown when I was learning my craft as a cook. Now I expect young cooks would wonder what lard and suet are!

Rapeseed oil, nutty, and rich in both taste and colour, is now being produced by Priors Byne Farm, near Partridge Green, which presses a great oil and sells it under the descriptive and apt name of Sussex Gold. It is cold-pressed for maximum purity and flavour – although I take issue with the label of extra virgin, a term which should only really be applied to olive oils, but that moan makes me gastro pedantic!

I first met the team from Priors Byne Farm at a food show at Olympia in London – so often you have to travel to meet your neighbours! I have been using their oil ever since and find it to have a clean, quite peppery and distinctively nutty taste, almost with a hint of coriander seed. It is fragrant when used for cooking, as are all cold-pressed oils, releasing its aroma as it is heated. It is also very thick and very yellow. The taste is distinctive and delicious, as good in cakes as it is in curries.

Rape ready for harvest looks like a crop left for too long, but the black seeds which contain the oil are held in long seed pods which develop as the fragrant flower heads fade. A key component of margarines, the oil was first marketed in its own right in the UK by Duncan Farringdon in Northamptonshire under the brand name Mellow Yellow. His success encouraged many regional oils into being, and Sussex Gold now boasts not only an oil but a range of sauces, dressings and mayonnaise too.

I often use the oil in bakes that are derived from carrot cakes. These are batter-like in consistency, easy to mix and always moist and a little bit different. Rapeseed oil is definitely an almost standard ingredient in the modern kitchen and we are lucky to have such a good local oil on our doorstep. Sussex Gold is in many supermarkets and farm shops, and is sold direct through farmers' markets across the county.

Courgette Cake with Lemon Butter Icing

Makes 1 large loaf cake

This is a splendid cake, not too sweet and it can be made with white or wholewheat flour. I use Sussex Gold rapeseed oil and have to confess that I prefer lemon to lime (the more trendy option) to flavour the icing. If you bake this as muffins they will take 20–25 minutes.

2 medium courgettes, about 200g
150g thick natural yogurt
2 large eggs
100ml rapeseed oil or similar
200g self-raising flour
1 tsp each bicarbonate of soda and ground ginger
150g light muscovado sugar
100g currants

For the icing:

Grated zest and juice of half a lemon
75g softened butter
150–200g icing sugar

1. Preheat the oven to gas mark 5/190°C. Line a loaf tin with baking parchment.

2. Trim the courgettes to give 200g, grate them coarsely and squeeze the water out of the shreds with your hand. Beat the eggs with the yogurt and oil.

3. Combine the dry ingredients in a large bowl. Add the squeezed courgettes then the eggy liquid and beat thoroughly until well blended with a wooden spoon. Continue to beat the mixture for 30–60 seconds once it has formed a thick batter. Spoon it carefully into the prepared tin.

4. Bake for about 45 minutes, until a skewer inserted into the centre of the cake comes out clean. Leave for a few minutes then remove from the tin and cool on a wire rack.

5. Finely grate the zest from the lemon and squeeze the juice into a bowl. Add the butter and sugar and beat well to a smooth icing. Spread thickly over the top of the cold cake.

West Sussex Pesto

I have described making a wild garlic pesto on page 120. This recipe is made completely from West Sussex-sourced ingredients (wet walnuts are available in the early autumn, usually in October) and can be your blueprint for creative pesto making.

1 bunch of watercress
1 large handful of parsley (optional)
1–2 cloves garlic
1 red chilli
40g Parmesan-style pasta cheese
40g walnuts, or more to taste
Rapeseed oil

1. Roughly chop the watercress and parsley, if used, and place in a blender. Peel the garlic, seed the chilli then roughly chop both. Grate the cheese.

2. Add all the ingredients to the blender with sufficient oil to allow everything to blend to a thick paste. Season to taste. Keep refrigerated and use as required.

Index

Notes

Notes

Notes

Notes

Notes

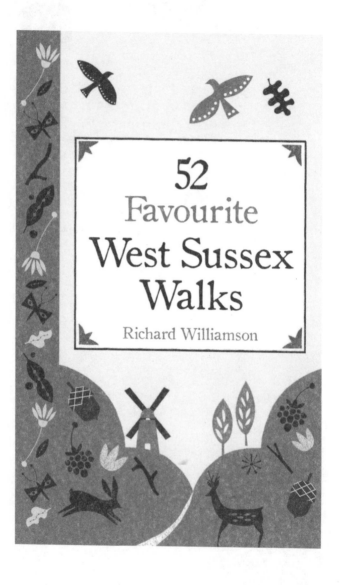

52
Favourite
West Sussex
Walks

Richard Williamson

52 FAVOURITE WEST SUSSEX WALKS

Richard Williamson

ISBN: 978 1 84953 233 4   Hardback   £9.99

Richard Williamson's weekly walking column has long been one of the most popular features in the *Chichester Observer* and *West Sussex Gazette*. Now, following the format that has proved such a hit over the years, for the first time he has compiled his favourite walks – one for every week of the year – with hand-drawn route maps. His knowledge and love of the timeless South Downs landscape and its varied flora, fauna and stories – from bat-birds and the Devil's Jumps to beloved pubs and famous poets – combine with practical notes on routes that can be covered easily in an afternoon.

Richard Williamson was for 30 years the manager of Kingley Vale National Nature Reserve and has an unparalleled knowledge of South Downs wildlife and lore.

'If you fancy a walk... all you need is this great pocket guide... there really is fun for all the family.'

PRIMARY TIMES

'His friendly, folksy style encourages the walker to revel in the journey and sights to be seen rather than regard it as a set task to be completed before nightfall...'

SUSSEX LIFE MAGAZINE

Have you enjoyed this book?
If so, why not write a review on your
favourite website?

If you're interested in finding out more about
our books, find us on Facebook at Summersdale
Publishers and follow us on Twitter at
@Summersdale.

Thanks very much for buying this
Summersdale book.

www.summersdale.com

www.feastofwestsussex.co.uk